ENVIRONMENTAL RESEARCH ADVANCES

FEDERAL LAND POLICY, RESOURCE MANAGEMENT, AGENCY APPROPRIATIONS AND REVENUES

ENVIRONMENTAL RESEARCH ADVANCES

Additional books in this series can be found on Nova's website under the Series tab.

Additional e-books in this series can be found on Nova's website under the e-book tab.

ENVIRONMENTAL RESEARCH ADVANCES

FEDERAL LAND POLICY, RESOURCE MANAGEMENT, AGENCY APPROPRIATIONS AND REVENUES

FELICIA MARTIN
EDITOR

nova publishers
New York

Library of Congress Cataloging-in-Publication Data

ISBN: 978-1-63482-168-1

Published by Nova Science Publishers, Inc. † New York

CONTENTS

PREFACE

This book introduces some of the broad themes and issues Congress considers when addressing federal land policy and resource management. This book also discusses appropriation and revenues of federal land management agencies.

Chapter 1 – The Property Clause in the U.S. Constitution (Article IV, § 3, Clause 2) grants Congress the authority to acquire, dispose of, and manage federal property. The 113th Congress is considering multiple federal land and natural resources policy and management issues. These issues are complex and often interrelated, and include how much and which land the government should own, and how lands and resources should be used and managed. These issues affect local communities, industries, ecosystems, and the nation.

Four agencies (referred to in this report as the federal land management agencies, or FLMAs) administer a total of 614 million surface acres (95%) of federal lands: the Forest Service (FS) in the Department of Agriculture (USDA), and the Bureau of Land Management (BLM), Fish and Wildlife Service (FWS), and National Park Service (NPS), all in the Department of the Interior (DOI). The federal estate also extends to the energy and mineral resources located below ground and offshore. These include about 700 million onshore acres of the federal subsurface mineral estate that are managed by BLM. In addition, the Bureau of Ocean Energy Management (BOEM), also in DOI, manages approximately 1.7 billion offshore acres located in federal waters within and beyond the U.S. Exclusive Economic Zone. Not all of these acres contain extractable mineral and energy resources.

This report introduces some of the broad themes and issues Congress considers when addressing federal land policy and resource management. Federal land policy includes questions about the extent and location of the federal estate. For example, some legislation in the 113th Congress would continue funding laws that authorize the acquisition of additional lands, while other legislation proposes conveying some land out of federal ownership or management. Other issues for Congress include whether certain lands or resources should have additional protections, for example, by designating certain lands as wilderness or national monuments, or protecting endangered species and their habitat. Congress may also address questions about wildfire management on both federal and nonfederal lands, including questions of how to fund suppression efforts.

Other policy questions involve how federal land should be used. Certain federal lands are considered primary- or dominant-use lands as specified in statute by Congress. For example, the primary-use mission of the National Wildlife Refuge System is to conserve plants and animals, and the dual-use mission of the National Park System is to conserve unique resources and provide for their use and enjoyment by the public. BLM and FS lands, however, have a statutory mission to balance multiple uses: recreation, grazing, timber, habitat and watershed protection, and energy production. Conflicts arise as users and land managers attempt to balance these uses both spatially and temporally. The 113th Congress has introduced several bills that would attempt to clarify and prioritize these uses. Some legislation would prioritize timber production, while other legislation would prioritize habitat or species conservation above other uses. Some legislation would ensure that all federal lands were accessible for hunting and fishing, while other legislation would ensure access to federal lands for energy development. In addition to questions about balancing energy production against other uses, other questions include how to balance traditional and alternative energy production on federal lands. Congress also considers how to charge for access and use of federal resources and lands, how to use those funds, and if and how to compensate local governments for the presence of untaxed federal lands within their borders. Title XXX of the FY2015 National Defense Authorization Act (H.R. 3979) contains a package of provisions related to federal land and natural resources management.

Chapter 2 – A perennial focus for Congress is on appropriations for management of federal lands and resources. Issues include the purposes for which appropriations are used, factors influencing their distribution among states, and the extent to which appropriations are used on nonfederal lands. Congress also continues to be interested in the revenues derived from federal lands and resources. Questions relate to the amount of revenue generated on federal lands, the sources of revenue, and factors affecting the variation among states in the amount and type of revenue generated.

Approximately 95% of federal lands are managed by four agencies: the Bureau of Land Management (BLM), Fish and Wildlife Service (FWS), National Park Service (NPS), and Forest Service (FS). Their FY2013 appropriations were $2,048.1 million for BLM, $2,591.6 million for FWS, $3,305.8 million for NPS, and $5,709.8 million for FS. Of these totals, FS received the largest discretionary appropriation ($4,934.7 million) while FWS had the highest mandatory appropriation ($1,053.1 million). The largest discretionary appropriation for FS was for Wildland Fire Management; for the other three agencies, it was the main operations account. The agencies have many sources of mandatory appropriations, some of which are common among them and across states (e.g., recreation fees) while others are unique to one agency or allocated to one state. Another distinction concerns the portion of appropriations used on lands not managed by the agencies, ranging from little in the case of BLM to roughly two-thirds for FWS.

Revenue collections during FY2013 differed among the agencies, with $18.9 million for FWS, $223.6 million for FS, $333.4 million for NPS, and $525.0 million for BLM. Depending on the agency and state, sources of revenue might include land sales, grazing, timber, hardrock minerals, recreation, and rights of way. Influencing the allocation of appropriations among states and the amount of revenue collected in each state were the acreage of federal land; land resources, conditions, availability, uses, and impacts; demographics; fire activity; and other factors.

BLM, FWS, NPS, and FS also receive federal lands highway funds from the Federal Highway Administration. A total of $573.8 million in highway funding for federal lands was distributed in FY2013, with almost half ($280.6 million) going to NPS and another two-fifths ($227.2 million) to state Programming Decisions Committees (bodies that make some project funding decisions). The remainder went to FWS ($36.5 million), FS ($19.8 million), and BLM ($9.6 million). Distributions among states ranged from less than $0.1 million to $86.5 million.

The Payments in Lieu of Taxes program and FS Payments to States program compensate local governments for the presence of federally owned land. PILT applies to many types of federal lands, and payments are calculated under a formula. The total PILT payment in FY2013 was $401.8 million, with state totals ranging from $0 to $41.4 million (for California). The FS Payments to States program—which includes Secure Rural Schools (SRS) payments—applies to counties with national forest lands and certain BLM forested lands. Payments are based on either historic or current revenue generated on the lands, and other considerations. FY2013 payments to states totaled $312.5 million, ranging from less than $0.1 million to $97.1 million (for Oregon).

The Department of the Interior's Office of Natural Resources Revenue (ONRR) collects mineral leasing revenues from all federal onshore areas. Revenue is derived from many commodities, including coal, gas, hardrock minerals, oil, phosphate, sodium, and sulfur. For FY2013, ONRR reported $4,296.9 million from federal lands in 37 states, with revenues by state of less than $0.1 million to $1,998.9 million (for Wyoming).

In: Federal Land Policy
Editor: Felicia Martin

ISBN: 978-1-63482-168-1

Chapter 1

FEDERAL LANDS AND NATURAL RESOURCES: OVERVIEW AND SELECTED ISSUES FOR THE 113TH CONGRESS*

Katie Hoover

SUMMARY

The Property Clause in the U.S. Constitution (Article IV, § 3, Clause 2) grants Congress the authority to acquire, dispose of, and manage federal property. The 113th Congress is considering multiple federal land and natural resources policy and management issues. These issues are complex and often interrelated, and include how much and which land the government should own, and how lands and resources should be used and managed. These issues affect local communities, industries, ecosystems, and the nation.

Four agencies (referred to in this report as the federal land management agencies, or FLMAs) administer a total of 614 million surface acres (95%) of federal lands: the Forest Service (FS) in the Department of Agriculture (USDA), and the Bureau of Land Management (BLM), Fish and Wildlife Service (FWS), and National Park Service (NPS), all in the Department of the Interior (DOI). The federal estate also extends to the energy and mineral resources located

* This is an edited, reformatted and augmented version of a Congressional Research Service publication R43429, prepared for Members and Committees of Congress, dated December 8, 2014.

below ground and offshore. These include about 700 million onshore acres of the federal subsurface mineral estate that are managed by BLM. In addition, the Bureau of Ocean Energy Management (BOEM), also in DOI, manages approximately 1.7 billion offshore acres located in federal waters within and beyond the U.S. Exclusive Economic Zone. Not all of these acres contain extractable mineral and energy resources.

This report introduces some of the broad themes and issues Congress considers when addressing federal land policy and resource management. Federal land policy includes questions about the extent and location of the federal estate. For example, some legislation in the 113th Congress would continue funding laws that authorize the acquisition of additional lands, while other legislation proposes conveying some land out of federal ownership or management. Other issues for Congress include whether certain lands or resources should have additional protections, for example, by designating certain lands as wilderness or national monuments, or protecting endangered species and their habitat. Congress may also address questions about wildfire management on both federal and nonfederal lands, including questions of how to fund suppression efforts.

Other policy questions involve how federal land should be used. Certain federal lands are considered primary- or dominant-use lands as specified in statute by Congress. For example, the primary-use mission of the National Wildlife Refuge System is to conserve plants and animals, and the dual-use mission of the National Park System is to conserve unique resources and provide for their use and enjoyment by the public. BLM and FS lands, however, have a statutory mission to balance multiple uses: recreation, grazing, timber, habitat and watershed protection, and energy production. Conflicts arise as users and land managers attempt to balance these uses both spatially and temporally. The 113th Congress has introduced several bills that would attempt to clarify and prioritize these uses. Some legislation would prioritize timber production, while other legislation would prioritize habitat or species conservation above other uses. Some legislation would ensure that all federal lands were accessible for hunting and fishing, while other legislation would ensure access to federal lands for energy development. In addition to questions about balancing energy production against other uses, other questions include how to balance traditional and alternative energy production on federal lands. Congress also considers how to charge for access and use of federal resources and lands, how to use those funds, and if and how to compensate local governments for the presence of untaxed federal lands within their borders. Title XXX of the FY2015 National Defense Authorization Act (H.R. 3979) contains a package of provisions related to federal land and natural resources management.

INTRODUCTION

Federal land management decisions influence the U.S. economy, environment, and social welfare. These decisions determine how the nation's federal lands will be acquired, developed, managed, and protected. Their impact may be local or regional, or may even rise to the national level. This report discusses selected federal land policy issues that the 113th Congress is addressing or may consider through oversight, authorizations, or appropriations. The report identifies CRS products that provide more detailed information.[1]

The federal government manages roughly 640 million acres of surface land, approximately 28% of the 2.3 billion acres of land in the United States.[2] Four agencies (referred to in this report as the federal land management agencies, or FLMAs) administer a total of 614 million acres (95%) of federal lands: the Forest Service (FS) in the Department of Agriculture (USDA), and the Bureau of Land Management (BLM), Fish and Wildlife Service (FWS), and National Park Service (NPS), all in the Department of the Interior (DOI). Most of these lands are in the West and Alaska, where the percentage of federal ownership is significantly higher than elsewhere in the nation (see *Figure 1*).[3] In addition, the Department of Defense administers 19 million acres in military bases, training ranges, and more; and numerous other agencies administer the remaining federal acreage.[4]

The federal estate also extends to the energy and mineral resources located below ground and offshore. These include about 700 million onshore acres of the federal subsurface mineral estate and about 1.7 billion acres located beyond state coastal waters—referred to as U.S. offshore areas—although not all of these acres contain extractable mineral and energy resources. The U.S. offshore areas, which lie within and beyond the U.S. Exclusive Economic Zone (EEZ), are also referred to as the Outer Continental Shelf (OCS). U.S. offshore areas represent approximately 4.5 million square miles, or an area about 23% larger than the total land area of the United States.

Federal land policy and management issues generally fall into several broad themes: Should federal land be managed to produce national or local benefits? How should current uses be balanced with future supplies and opportunities? Should current uses, management, and protection programs be replaced with alternatives? Who decides how federal land resources should be managed, and how are the decisions made? Some stakeholders seek to maintain or enhance the federal estate, while others seek to divest the federal estate to state or private ownership. Some issues, such as forest management and fire protection, involve both federal and nonfederal (state, local, or privately owned) land. In many cases, federal land issues do not divide along clear party lines. Instead, they may be split along the lines of rural-urban, eastern-western, and coastal-interior interests.

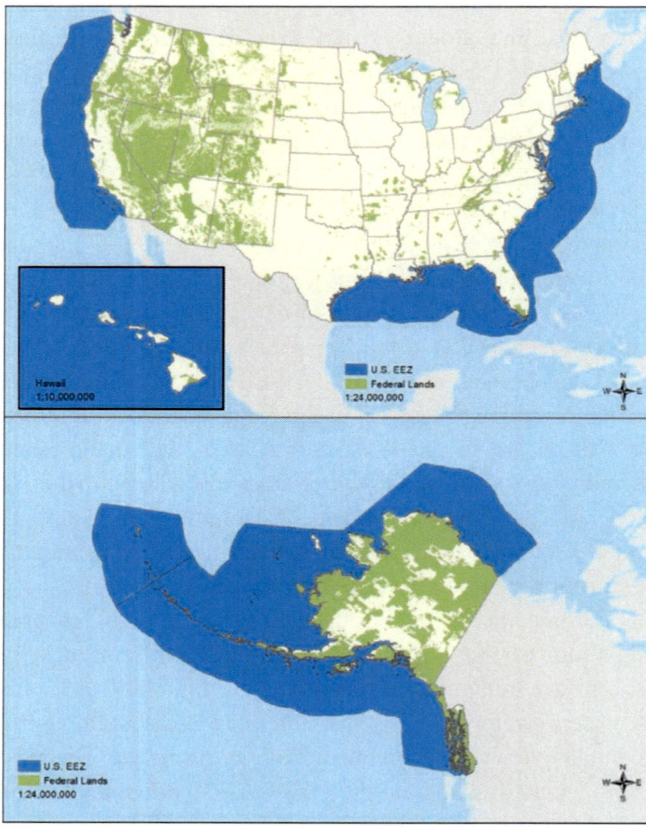

Source: CRS.

Notes: Federal lands in this figure include only the approximately 614 million acres of surface federal lands managed by the FLMAs. It is not uncommon to see statutory references to "federal waters," "U.S. EEZ" and "U.S. OCS." These terms might be used interchangeably in some policy contexts; however, most experts caution that each term can refer to a distinct geographical area. This map shows a generalized image of federal lands and submerged lands without attempting to demonstrate with any specificity the geographical area of the U.S. EEZ as defined by state or federal courts, lawmakers, or agency officials.

Figure 1. Federal Onshore and Offshore Management Areas.

Several authorizing committees in the House and Senate have jurisdiction over myriad federal lands issues. For example, issues involving the management of the national forests cross multiple committee jurisdictions. In addition, federal land issues are often addressed during consideration of annual appropriations for the FLMAs' programs and activities.

This report introduces selected federal land issues, many of which are complex and interrelated. The discussions are broad and aim to introduce the reader to the range of issues regarding federal land management, while providing references to more detailed and specific CRS products available on the issue. After a background section on the FLMAs, the issues are grouped into 10 broad categories:

- Federal Estate Ownership
- Funding for Federal Land Management
- Climate Management
- Offshore Federal Lands
- Onshore Energy and Minerals Resources and Development
- Range Management
- Recreation on Federal Lands
- Special Land Designations
- Species Management
- Wildfire Management

THE FEDERAL LAND MANAGEMENT AGENCIES (FLMAS)

Federal land ownership began when the original 13 states ceded title of some of their land to the newly formed central government.[5] The early federal policy was to dispose of federal land to generate revenue and encourage western settlement and development. However, Congress began to withdraw, reserve, and protect federal land through the creation of national parks and forest reserves starting in the late 1800s. The "reservation era" laid the foundation for the current federal agencies, whose primary purpose is to manage natural resources on federal lands.

The four federal land management agencies (FLMAs)—the Forest Service, the National Park Service, the Fish and Wildlife Service, and the Bureau of Land Management—administer about 95%-96% (614 million acres) of the 635-640 million acres of surface federal land,[6] and an additional 700 million acres of subsurface federal mineral estate (although not all of these acres contain extractable mineral and energy resources). In addition to the FLMAs, the Bureau of Ocean Energy Management administers nearly 2 billion acres of offshore federal submerged lands. These five agencies were created at different times, with different missions and purposes as discussed below, and are authorized in several different House and Senate committees. However, these agencies all receive funding through the annual Interior, Environment, and Related Agencies appropriations laws, as well as through various trust funds and special accounts.

Forest Service

The Forest Service (FS) is the oldest of the federal land management agencies. Although the first forest reserves—later renamed national forests—were created in 1891, the FS was established later, in 1905 in the Department of Agriculture. The FS is charged with managing the national forest system, as well as conducting forestry research and providing assistance to state and private forest owners. Today, FS administers nearly 193 million acres of land—including 155 national forests and 20 national grasslands—predominately in the West (although FS manages more than half of all the eastern federal lands).

The forest reserves were originally authorized to protect the lands, preserve water flows, and provide timber. These purposes were expanded in the Multiple-Use Sustained-Yield Act of 1960.[7] This act added recreation, livestock grazing, and wildlife and fish habitat as purposes of the national forests, with wilderness added as a defined management objective in 1964.[8] The act directed that these multiple uses be managed in a "harmonious and coordinated" manner and "in the combination that will best meet the needs of the American people." The act also directed the FS to manage the renewable resources under the principle of sustained yield, meaning to achieve a high level of resource outputs in perpetuity, without impairing the productivity of the lands. Congress reaffirmed and expanded the multiple-use sustained-yield management directive in subsequent legislation, including the Forest Rangeland Renewable Resources Planning Act of 1974 (RPA)[9] and the National Forest Management Act of 1976 (NFMA).[10] The RPA and NFMA also direct the FS to conduct long-range planning efforts to manage the national forests. Balancing the multiple uses across the national forest system has sometimes led to conflicts regarding management decisions and priorities.

Bureau of Land Management

The BLM was formed in 1946 by combining two existing agencies.[11] The BLM currently administers more onshore federal lands than any other agency—247 million acres. BLM lands are heavily concentrated (99.8%) in the 12 western states. Nearly half of the total acreage is in two states—Alaska (29%) and Nevada (19%). BLM lands, officially designated the National System of Public Lands, include grasslands, forests, high mountains, arctic tundra, and deserts. BLM lands often are intermingled with other federal or private lands, and the agency has authority to acquire, dispose of, and exchange lands under various authorities.

As defined in the Federal Land Policy and Management Act of 1976 (FLPMA),[12] BLM management responsibilities are similar to those of the FS—sustained yields of the multiple uses, including recreation, grazing, timber, watershed, wildlife and fish habitat, and conservation. For instance, about 156 million acres are available for livestock grazing, and about 27 million acres are in BLM's National Landscape Conservation System. Some lands are withdrawn (restricted) from one or more uses, or managed for a predominant use. The agency inventories its lands and resources and develops land use plans for its land units. In addition, BLM administers onshore federal energy and mineral resources, covering nearly 700 million acres of federal subsurface mineral estate, although not all of these acres contain extractable mineral and energy resources. BLM also supervises the mineral operations on about 56 million acres of Indian trust lands. Conflicts sometimes arise among and between users and land managers as a result of the diversity of the lands and multiple use opportunities provided on BLM public lands.

Fish and Wildlife Service

The first national wildlife refuge was established by executive order in 1903. In 1966 the refuges were aggregated into the National Wildlife Refuge System, administered by the Fish and Wildlife Service (FWS). Today, the FWS administers 89 million acres of federal land, of which 77 million acres (86%) are in Alaska.[13] The FWS also administers several largely marine refuges around Hawaii and U.S. territories in the Pacific (53 million acres total). Several large marine national monuments[14] are also administered by the FWS, but are not part of the National Wildlife Refuge System—they include the Papahanaumokuakea National Monument (89 million acres in Hawaii), the

Rose Atoll National Monument (9 million acres in American Samoa), the Marianas Trench National Monument (10 million acres), and the Pacific Remote Islands Marine National Monument (49 million acres).

In contrast to the multiple-use missions of FS and BLM, the FWS has a primary-use mission—to conserve plants and animals. Other uses (motorized recreation, timber cutting, grazing, etc.) are permitted, to the extent that they are compatible with the species' needs, but wildlife-related activities (hunting, bird-watching, hiking, education, etc.) are considered "priority uses" and are given preference over consumptive uses such as timber, grazing, and minerals. Determining compatibility can be challenging, but the relative clarity of the mission generally has minimized conflicts over refuge management and use.

National Park Service

The National Park Service (NPS) was created in 1916[15] to manage the growing number of park units established by Congress and monuments proclaimed by the President. The national park system has grown to 401 units with diverse titles—national park, national monument, national preserve, national historic site, national recreation area, national battlefield, and many more.[16] The Park Service administers 85 million acres of federal land in all 50 states, the District of Columbia, and U.S. territories. Roughly two-thirds of the system's lands are in Alaska.[17]

The NPS has a dual mission—to preserve unique resources and to provide for their enjoyment by the public. Park units include spectacular natural areas (e.g., Yellowstone, Grand Canyon, and Arches National Parks), unique prehistoric sites (e.g., Mesa Verde National Park and Dinosaur National Monument), and special places in American history (e.g., Valley Forge National Historic Park, Gettysburg National Military Park, and the Statue of Liberty National Monument), as well as areas that focus on recreation (e.g., Cape Cod National Seashore and Glen Canyon National Recreation Area). NPS laws, regulations, and policies emphasize the conservation of park resources in conservation/use conflicts, and the system's lands and resources generally receive a higher level of protection than those of the BLM and the FS. The tension between providing recreation and preserving resources has produced many management challenges for the Park Service.

Bureau of Ocean Energy Management

The Bureau of Ocean Energy Management (BOEM) was established in 2010 as part of the federal response to the *Deepwater Horizon* oil spill.[18] Specifically, BOEM was created as part of DOI structural reforms to replace the Minerals Management Service (MMS), which was previously responsible for managing offshore energy resources.[19] BOEM's mission is to balance energy independence, environmental protection, and economic development through responsible, science-based management of offshore conventional and renewable energy resources in four regions: Atlantic, Pacific, Gulf of Mexico, and the Arctic (see *Figure 1*).

BOEM prepares and maintains a schedule of proposed oil and gas lease sales,[20] issues easements and leases for deploying renewable energy technologies,[21] and manages ownership records for offshore tracts leased for energy development. Furthermore, BOEM administers offshore sand and gravel resources to assist state beach replenishment efforts. OCS revenues are allocated mainly to two federal programs—the Land and Water Conservation Fund and the Historic Preservation Fund.[22]

BOEM manages energy resources in areas covering approximately 1.7 billion acres located beyond state waters and comprising areas defined in the Outer Continental Shelf (OCS) Lands Act, as amended in 1978 (OCSLA).[23] Most OCS acreage is concentrated in the Alaska region (approximately 1.03 billion acres), but some OCS acreage exists off all coastal states.[24] Because of the cross-cutting nature of its management responsibilities, BOEM shares some responsibilities with two other DOI agencies: the Bureau of Safety and Environmental Enforcement (BSEE) and the Office of Natural Resources Revenue (ONRR).[25]

CRS Products

CRS Report R42346, *Federal Land Ownership: Overview and Data*, by Carol Hardy Vincent, Laura A. Hanson, and Marc R. Rosenblum.

CRS Report R40225, *Federal Land Management Agencies: Background on Land and Resources Management.*

CRS Report RL34267, *Federal Land Ownership: Constitutional Authority and the History of Acquisition, Disposal, and Retention*, by Kristina Alexander.

CRS Report R42656, *Federal Land Management Agencies and Programs: CRS Experts*, by Katie Hoover.

CRS Report R43137, *Department of the Interior Ocean Energy Bureaus: Status of 2010 Structural Reforms and Issues for Congress*, by Curry L. Hagerty.

FEDERAL ESTATE OWNERSHIP

The ownership and use of federal lands has generated controversy for decades. One key area of debate is the extent of the federal estate; or, in other words, how much land the federal government should own (*Figure 1*). This debate includes questions about disposing of some federal land to state or private ownership, or if additional land should be acquired for conservation, open space, or other purposes. For lands retained in federal ownership, questions have centered around whether to curtail certain land designations (e.g., national monuments proclaimed by the President or special management areas established by Congress) or if current management procedures should be changed (e.g., to allow a greater role for state and local governments or to expand economic considerations in decision-making). A separate issue is how to ensure the security of international borders along the federal lands, which are managed by multiple agencies.

The Property Clause in the U.S. Constitution (Article IV, § 3, Clause 2) grants Congress authority over federal property, and the Supreme Court has described Congress's power to legislate under this clause as "without limitation." Congress has granted the FLMAs varying and limited authorities to acquire and dispose of land. The extent of this authority varies considerably among the FLMAs. The BLM has relatively broad authority for both acquisitions and disposals under the FLPMA. By contrast, the NPS has almost no general authority to acquire land to create new park units or to dispose of park lands without congressional action. The FS authority to acquire lands is mostly limited to lands within or contiguous to the boundaries of a national forest. The agency has various authorities to dispose of land, but they are relatively constrained and infrequently used. The FWS has various authorities to acquire lands, but no general authority to dispose of its lands. For example, the Migratory Bird Conservation Act of 1929 grants the FWS authority to acquire land for the National Wildlife Refuge System—in part using funds from the sale of hunting and conservation stamps—after state consultation and agreement.[26]

The current acquisition and disposal authorities form the backdrop for consideration of measures to establish, modify, or eliminate authorities, or to provide for the acquisition or disposal of particular lands. Congress also addresses acquisition and disposal policy in the context of debates on the role and goals of the federal government in owning and managing land generally, and has considered broader measures to dispose of lands or to promote acquisition.

CRS Products

CRS Report R42346, *Federal Land Ownership: Overview and Data*, by Carol Hardy Vincent, Laura A. Hanson, and Marc R. Rosenblum.

CRS Report RL34273, *Federal Land Ownership: Acquisition and Disposal Authorities*, by Carol Hardy Vincent et al..

CRS Report RL34267, *Federal Land Ownership: Constitutional Authority and the History of Acquisition, Disposal, and Retention*, by Kristina Alexander.

CRS Report R41770, *Leasing and Selling Federal Lands and Resources: Receipts and Their Disposition*, by Carol Hardy Vincent and Marc Humphries.

FUNDING FOR FEDERAL LANDS

Funding for federal land and natural resource programs presents an array of issues for Congress. Most of the FLMAs receive appropriations through the Interior, Environment, and Related Agencies appropriations bill.[27] In addition to questions related directly to appropriations, other funding questions relate to the compensation of counties for the presence of federal lands, including whether to revise or maintain existing payment programs. A second set of questions relates to the Land and Water Conservation Fund, from which Congress appropriates funds for land acquisition by federal agencies, outdoor recreation needs of states, and other purposes. Under debate are the levels, sources, and uses of funding and whether the funding should be reauthorized and continued as discretionary. A third set of issues relates to the maintenance of assets by the agencies, particularly how to address their backlog of maintenance projects while achieving other government priorities.

Federal Payment Programs

As a condition of statehood, most states forever waived the right to tax federal lands within their borders. However, some believe federal lands may create demand for services such as fire protection, police cooperation, or longer roads to skirt the federal property. Under federal law, local governments are compensated through various programs due to the presence of federally owned land. Some of these programs are run by specific agencies and apply only to that agency's land. In addition, portions of the rents and royalties charged for energy development and production on both onshore and offshore federal lands may be shared with the states or local governments where the land or mineral deposit is located.

The most widely applicable program, administered by the DOI, applies to many types of federally owned land, and is called "Payments in Lieu of Taxes," or PILT. Counties with NPS lands primarily receive payments under PILT. The FS and BLM have additional payment programs based primarily on receipts from revenue-producing activities on their lands; FWS has a smaller payment program for certain refuge lands. One program (Secure Rural Schools or SRS) compensates counties with National Forest System lands or certain BLM lands in Oregon for declining timber harvests. The adequacy, coverage, and equity of the payment formulas for all of these programs are recurring issues for Congress, particularly in the case of SRS and PILT payments.

CRS Products

CRS Report R42439, Compensating State and Local Governments for the Tax-Exempt Status of Federal Lands: What Is Fair and Consistent?, by M. Lynne Corn.

CRS Report RL31392, PILT (Payments in Lieu of Taxes): Somewhat Simplified, by M. Lynne Corn.

CRS Report R41303, Reauthorizing the Secure Rural Schools and Community Self-Determination Act of 2000, by Katie Hoover.

CRS Report R42404, Fish and Wildlife Service: Compensation to Local Governments, by M. Lynne Corn.

CRS Report R42951, The Oregon & California Railroad Lands (O&C Lands): Issues for Congress, by Katie Hoover.

Land and Water Conservation Fund

The Land and Water Conservation Fund Act of 1965 was enacted to help preserve, develop, and assure access to outdoor recreation facilities to strengthen the health of U.S. citizens. The law created the Land and Water

Conservation Fund (LWCF) in the U.S. Treasury as a funding source to implement its outdoor recreation purposes. The LWCF has been the principal source of monies for land acquisition for outdoor recreation by the four FLMAs. The LWCF also has funded a matching grant program to assist states in recreational planning, acquiring recreational lands and waters, and developing outdoor recreational facilities. Further, LWCF has been used to fund other federal programs with purposes related to lands and resources.

The LWCF is authorized at $900 million annually through September 30, 2015. While the fund accrues revenues and collections from multiple sources, nearly all of the revenues are derived from oil and gas leasing in the OCS. Congress determines the level of appropriations each year, and yearly appropriations have fluctuated widely since the origin of the program.[28] Of the total revenues that have accrued throughout the history of the program ($36.2 billion), less than half have been appropriated ($16.8 billion).[29]

There is a difference of opinion as to the appropriate level of funds for LWCF and how those funds should be used. Current congressional issues include deciding the amount to appropriate for land acquisition, the state grant program, and other purposes and whether to alter the processes for allocating acquisition funds and state grants. The primary context for debating these issues is annual Interior appropriations legislation. Several other issues have been under debate, including whether to reauthorize the LWCF beyond 2015; to provide the fund with permanent appropriations at the authorized level; to direct revenues from additional activities to the LWCF; to limit the use of funds for particular purposes, or, alternatively, to require some of the funds to be used for certain purposes; and to prohibit the disposal of, or limit the use of, lands acquired with LWCF monies.

CRS Product

CRS Report RL33531, Land and Water Conservation Fund: Overview, Funding History, and Issues, by Carol Hardy Vincent.

Deferred Maintenance

The FLMAs have maintenance responsibility for their buildings, roads and trails, recreation sites, and other infrastructure. Congress continues to focus on the agencies' deferred maintenance, often called the maintenance backlog, defined as maintenance that "was not performed when it should have been or was scheduled to be and which, therefore, is put off or delayed for a future period."[30] The agencies assert that continuing to defer maintenance of facilities accelerates their rate of deterioration, increases their repair costs, and decreases their value.

Congressional and administrative attention has centered on the NPS backlog, which has continued to increase from a FY1999 estimate of $4.25 billion. Currently, DOI estimates deferred maintenance for the NPS for FY2013 between $9.12 billion and $13.42 billion, with a mid-range figure of $11.27 billion. A majority of the backlogged maintenance (58%) is for roads, bridges, and trails. The other FLMAs also have maintenance backlogs. DOI estimates deferred maintenance for FY2013 for the FWS at between $1.63 billion and $2.39 billion and the BLM backlog at between $0.67 billion and $0.82 billion. The FS estimated its backlog for FY2012 at $6.03 billion.[31] Thus, the four agencies together had a combined backlog estimated at between $17.45 billion and $22.65 billion, with a mid-range figure of $20.05 billion.

The backlogs have been attributed to decades of funding shortfalls to address capital improvement projects. However, it is not clear how much total funding is provided for deferred maintenance each year because annual presidential budget requests and appropriations documents typically do not identify and aggregate all funds for deferred maintenance. Currently, there is debate over the appropriate level of funds to maintain infrastructure, whether to use funds from other programs/sources, how to balance maintenance of the existing infrastructure with the acquisition of new assets, and the priority of maintaining infrastructure relative to other government functions.

CLIMATE CHANGE AND FEDERAL LAND MANAGEMENT

Scientific evidence shows that the United States' climate has been changing in recent decades.[32] This poses several interrelated and complex issues for the management of federal lands and resources, in terms of mitigation, adaptation, and resiliency. Overall, climate change is introducing uncertainty about conditions previously considered relatively stable and predictable. Given the diversity of federal land and resources, concerns are wide-ranging and include, among other things, invasive species, sea-level rise, wildlife habitat changes, and vulnerability to extreme weather events, as well as concerns about the effects of these changes on tourism and recreation. More specific observed impacts include a fire season that begins earlier and lasts longer, warmer winter temperatures that allow various insect and disease infestations to persist, thinner snowpacks that melt earlier and contribute to drought conditions, and habitat shifts that may or may not exacerbate the status of sensitive species. Another concern is how climate change may impact some iconic federal lands, such as the diminishing size of the glaciers that cover Glacier National Park and several parks in Alaska,[33] or the flooding of some wildlife refuges.

The role of the federal government in responding to climate change is currently under debate. Some stakeholders see future climate conditions as representing an increased risk to the effective performance of the FLMAs' missions and roles. Others are concerned that a focus on climate change adaptations may divert resources and attention from other agency activities and near-term challenges. The debate largely hinges on how to make investments that will cost-effectively assist the agencies in successfully performing their activities in the near term and in future decades.

A related debate is the role of federal agencies—particularly the BLM and BOEM—in energy production on federal lands. Specifically in question is the extent to which the agencies should provide access to and promote the different sources of energy production. Both traditional sources of energy (non-renewable fossil fuels such as oil, gas, and coal) and alternative sources of energy (renewable fuels such as solar, wind, and geothermal) are available on federal lands. However, since fossil fuel emissions contribute to climate change, some argue that the agencies should prioritize renewable energy production on federal lands over traditional energy sources.

Several Administration-led efforts have been undertaken to prepare for the evolving climate change challenges facing federal land managers. In 2013, President Obama released a Climate Change Action Plan, which thus far has comprised a series of executive actions aimed to "reduce carbon pollution, prepare the United States for the impacts of climate change, and lead international efforts to address global climate change."[34] As part of the effort, the President established goals for renewable energy permitting on federal lands (discussed in more detail in the "Renewable Energy " section of this report). In Executive Order 13514 (2009), all federal agencies were instructed to participate actively to develop "approaches through which the policies and practices of the agencies can be made compatible with and reinforce" a national climate change adaptation strategy.[35] Further, the Council on Environmental Quality proposed draft guidance in 2010 on how federal agencies should consider the potential impacts of agency actions on climate change during the environmental review process required by the National Environmental Policy Act (NEPA).[36]

GAO Reports on Climate Change and Federal Land Management

Various Adaptation Efforts Are Underway at Key Natural Resource Management Agencies, GAO-13-253, May 31, 2013, http://www.gao.gov/products/gao-13-253.

Climate Change: Future Federal Adaptation Efforts Could Better Support Local Infrastructure Decision Makers, GAO-13-242, April 12, 2013, http://www.gao.gov/products/gao-13-242.

High Risk Series: An Update. GAO-13-359T, February 14, 2013, http://www.gao.gov/highrisk.

Climate Change: Agencies Should Develop Guidance for Addressing the Effects on Federal Land and Water Resources, GAO-07-863, August 7, 2007, http://www.gao.gov/products/GAO-07-863.

Adaptation: Strategic Federal Planning Could Help Government Officials Make More Informed Decisions, GAO-10-113, October 7, 2009, http://www.gao.gov/products/GAO-10-113.

The implementation status of FLMA adaptation efforts and their impact on operations and decision-making vary across the agencies. Some activities, such as those targeted at managing risk and integrating adaptive decision frameworks into decision-making, may now be incorporated as elements into climate change adaptation strategies and plans. A Government Accountability Office (GAO) report found federal resource managers were not prioritizing how climate change was already affecting, and may continue to affect, the resources for which they were responsible, and cited among the challenges that government officials face in their efforts to adapt to climate change: competing priorities, lack of guidance, insufficient site-specific data, and uncertainties about future change.[37] A survey of federal land managers found that the most common climate change actions that had been implemented fell into the following categories: public information and education, limiting or reducing emissions, forest thinning or fuel reduction, and additional measures to protect wildlife.[38]

Congress is addressing agency climate change efforts through appropriations, oversight, and legislation. Issues for Congress include whether additional statutes, regulations, or guidance for climate change is needed. More specific legislative issues for Congress may be the extent to which federal resources support a strategy to achieve long-term climate change policy goals, the demands of climate change programming for the FLMAs and the resources they manage, proposals to restructure or improve collaboration among the FLMAs regarding climate change activities, and possible reporting requirements to support congressional decision-making and oversight.

CRS Products

CRS Report R43230, Climate Change Legislation in the 113th Congress, by Jonathan L. Ramseur.

CRS Report R43227, Federal Climate Change Funding from FY2008 to FY2014, by Jane A. Leggett, Richard K. Lattanzio, and Emily Bruner.

CRS Report R43229, Climate Change Science: Key Points, by Jane A. Leggett.

CRS Report R43120, President Obama's Climate Action Plan, coordinated by Jane A. Leggett. CRS Report R41144, Deforestation and Climate Change, by Pervaze A. Sheikh.

CRS Report R41691, Forest Management for Resilience and Adaptation, by Pervaze A. Sheikh.

OFFSHORE FEDERAL RESOURCES

Since 1978, the cornerstone of managing offshore federal resources within and beyond the U.S. EEZ has been the mandate to consider two national interests: meeting domestic energy demands and protecting the environment.[39] Historically, public concern about U.S. dependence on foreign fuels and about vulnerability of shoreline communities to oil-spill risks has prompted policymakers to debate allowing access to certain ocean areas for offshore drilling.[40] This debate has a complicated and controversial history. Those in favor of protecting marine and coastal areas from oil-spill risks support banning drilling through moratoriums, non-development zones, and other measures. Others claim that reducing the nation's dependence on foreign sources requires increasing offshore oil and gas development to strengthen and diversify the nation's domestic energy portfolio, and the drilling can be done in a safe manner that protects marine and coastal areas. A related theme is the tension over whether access should be granted or deferred in certain ocean areas.

Energy Resources

The federal government's ocean energy resource management responsibilities are national in scope, covering vast ocean areas belonging to the United States (see *Figure 1*). Since 2005, when Congress clarified federal authority for managing ocean renewable energy resources, BOEM has been in the process of estimating renewable ocean energy resources to facilitate electricity generation from offshore wind, thermal power, and kinetic forces from ocean tides and waves.[41] According to the Energy Information Administration, by 2015 offshore wind projects are anticipated to have 200 MW of offshore wind capacity, producing about 750 million kWh per year of electricity.[42] These estimates contribute to resource management decisions in two different BOEM programs: the Offshore Renewable Energy Program[43] and the Five-Year OCS Oil and Gas Leasing Program.[44] No leases are yet producing within the Offshore Renewable Energy Program; BOEM administers over 6,000 leases within the oil and gas program.[45]

BOEM weighs environmental protection with the growing domestic energy needs through a multi-step process requiring consideration of a variety of water-dependent activities (military operations, fishing, shipping, tourism, and conservation).[46] Given the persistence of this balancing process, the 113th Congress has faced some perennial (and unresolved) questions. Are statutory changes needed to improve management of ocean energy resources? If so, what measures might be called for; and where and how would such measures be implemented? How might statutory changes to allow or defer access to ocean areas affect oil-spill risks, if at all? How might such changes affect energy supplies? What potential gains or losses might stem from such changes with respect to future receipts and disbursements from offshore projects?

CRS Products

CRS Report R40175, *Wind Energy: Offshore Permitting*, by Adam Vann.

CRS Report RL33404, *Offshore Oil and Gas Development: Legal Framework*, by Adam Vann.

CRS Report R41132, *Outer Continental Shelf Moratoria on Oil and Gas Development*, by Curry

L. Hagerty.

CRS Report R40645, *U.S. Offshore Oil and Gas Resources: Prospects and Processes*, by Marc Humphries and Robert Pirog.

Special Marine Designations

Congress has the authority to designate marine national monuments, as well as marine areas of special significance. For example, areas may be identified as marine sanctuaries pursuant to the National Marine Sanctuary Act (NMSA).[47] Marine sanctuaries range in size from less than one square mile to more than 137,792 square miles. The National Oceanic and Atmospheric Administration (NOAA)—an agency within the Department of Commerce—is responsible for managing 14 of these protected areas. Through the NMSA, activities are identified that can and cannot occur within the sanctuaries, sometimes in conjunction with state agencies or international organizations.[48] Some activities, such as research, may be permitted on a seasonal basis. Other special marine designations include marine protected areas (MPAs) and marine reserves. In these areas, some uses—particularly extractive uses such as fishing and oil and gas development—can be restricted or prohibited (also referred to as "no-take" areas), at times attracting controversy.

CRS Product

CRS Report RL32154, *Marine Protected Areas: An Overview*, by Harold F. Upton.

ONSHORE FEDERAL ENERGY AND MINERAL RESOURCES

Much of the federal estate is open to mineral exploration and development, including most BLM and many FS lands. However, NPS lands, areas within the National Wilderness Preservation System, and certain other federal lands have been specifically withdrawn from exploration and development. Recent concerns over energy supply and pricing have led some to look increasingly to federal lands as a potential energy source, for both traditional sources of energy and renewable energy projects. Balancing energy and mineral development and environmental protection is a perennial issue in managing federal lands. Another issue is if—and how much—the federal government should charge for these resources.

CRS Products

CRS Report R42756, *Energy Policy: 113th Congress Issues*, by Carl E. Behrens.

CRS Report R41770, *Leasing and Selling Federal Lands and Resources: Receipts and Their Disposition*, by Carol Hardy Vincent and Marc Humphries.

Oil, Natural Gas, and Coal

Oil and natural gas produced on federal lands account for 5% and 13% of total U.S. oil and gas production, respectively.[49] Congressional interest in these issues has focused on access to federal lands, the permitting process and timeline, how much to charge for leases and royalties, revenue collections, and how to balance environmental concerns. Development of oil, gas, and coal on federal lands is governed primarily by the Mineral Leasing Act of 1920 (MLA).[50] The MLA authorizes the Secretary of the Interior—through the BLM—to lease the subsurface rights to virtually all BLM and FS lands that contain fossil fuel deposits, with the federal government retaining title to the lands.[51] The MLA authorizes both competitive and noncompetitive bidding processes for oil and gas exploration and production leases, and competitive bidding for most coal leases. Leases include an annual rental fee and a royalty payment generally determined by a percentage of the value or amount of the resource removed or sold from the federal land. In addition, the Energy Policy Act of 2005 (EPAct05)[52] includes provisions governing access, leasing, and management of energy development on BLM and FS lands.[53]

Access to federal lands and permitting projects for energy and mineral development have been controversial issues. In 2008, BLM had 113 million acres of onshore federal lands open and accessible for oil and gas development, and about 166 million acres were off-limits or inaccessible.[54] The oil and gas industry contends that entry into the currently unavailable areas is necessary to ensure future domestic oil and gas supplies. Opponents maintain that the restricted lands are unique or environmentally sensitive and that the United States could realize equivalent energy gains through conservation and increased exploration on current leases or elsewhere. A related access issue is the extent to which BLM or FS may regulate hydraulic fracturing on federal lands. BLM has proposed two different draft rules—one in 2012 and then a revision in 2013—but has not issued final regulations as of publication of this report.[55] The proposed regulations would also extend to national forests, although FS is also debating this issue during the forest planning process at the individual unit level.

Another controversial issue is the permitting process and timeline, which EPAct05 revised for oil and gas permits. Although the time it takes BLM to process applications has decreased since FY2006, the time it takes applicants to respond and resolve issues with the applications has increased over that time period.[56] EPAct05 also authorized a pilot project to improve efficiency of processing oil and gas permits through FY2015.[57] After three years of implementation, a 2008 BLM report described improved interagency communication and a reduction in the time needed to review and process permit applications in the pilot locations.

Forty-three percent of U.S.-produced coal comes from federal lands. As a result, there are several congressional concerns, such as how to balance coal production against other resource values for federal lands. Other concerns include how to assess the value of the coal resource, what is the fair market value for the coal and what should be the government's royalty. In response to these congressional concerns, a 2013 GAO analysis found inconsistencies in how BLM evaluated and documented federal coal leases.[58] In addition, a 2013 DOI Inspector General report found BLM may have violated provisions in the MLA by accepting below-cost bids for federal coal leases.[59]

CRS Products

CRS Report R40806, Energy Projects on Federal Lands: Leasing and Authorization, by Adam Vann.

CRS Report R42432, U.S. Crude Oil and Natural Gas Production in Federal and Non-Federal Areas, by Marc Humphries.

Renewable Energy Sources

Concern over the impact of emissions from fossil fuel-fired power plants has resulted in increased interest in renewable energy sources. Interest in renewable energy sources has also been driven by the increasing adoption of statewide renewable portfolio standards that require electricity producers to supply a certain minimum share of electricity from renewable sources.[60] Both BLM and FS manage land that is considered suitable for renewable energy generation, and as such have authorized projects for geothermal, wind, solar, and biomass energy projects. Congressional interest in renewable energy resources on federal lands has focused on access, the permitting and leasing process, how much to charge for leases and royalties, market development, and how to balance environmental concerns with the development and production of these resources. These environmental concerns include wildlife impacts from wind turbines and water supply requirements for solar energy. In addition, some in Congress are interested in establishing a separate leasing system for managing solar and wind energy projects.

CRS Product

CRS Report R40806, Energy Projects on Federal Lands: Leasing and Authorization, by Adam Vann.

Geothermal Energy

One renewable energy source is geothermal energy, which is energy produced from heat stored under the surface of the earth. Geothermal leasing on federal lands is conducted under the authority of the Geothermal Steam Act of 1970, as amended.[61] BLM has the delegated authority for managing the permitting and leasing geothermal requirements for federal lands, in consultation with FS. In 2008, BLM and FS released a record of decision making 110 million acres of BLM public lands and 79 million acres of National Forest System lands available for leasing and potential development, pending site-specific analysis of future leasing applications.[62] The BLM manages 818 geothermal leases (59 in producing status), with a total capacity of 1,500 megawatts (about 40% of U.S. geothermal energy capacity). Under EPAct05, states receive 50% of the revenue generated from rental and royalty payments from geothermal leases within their states, counties receive 25%, and the remaining 25% goes to the Treasury. The Obama Administration has proposed returning to the pre-EPAct05 formula, which shared revenues equally among the states and the federal treasury.[63]

Wind and Solar Energy

Development of solar and wind energy sources on BLM and FS lands are governed by right-of-way authorities under Title V of FLPMA.[64] These projects could require large tracts of land to replace or add significant electric generating capacity, in addition to new transmission capacity. The extent of some of the environmental impacts of renewable energy production, such as impacts on wildlife and on environmentally sensitive areas, remains controversial. Also at issue for Congress is how to balance solar and wind project applications against other land uses. For example, in 2013, BLM finalized a rule allowing temporary withdrawal of subsurface mineral claims in areas with pending wind and solar project applications.[65]

BLM manages 20.6 million acres of public lands with wind energy potential and about 19 million acres for solar power development. As of September 2013, BLM has authorized 39 wind energy development projects and over 100 wind energy testing sites, and had 29 wind energy development applications pending on its public lands.[66] In October 2012, BLM finalized the plan for solar energy development on federal lands in six western states.[67] The Western Solar Plan established 19 Solar Energy Zones (SEZs) covering over 285,000 acres of federal lands that are designated as a priority area for commercial-scale solar projects. An October 2013 competitive auction to develop these projects received zero bids.[68] However, according to BLM, the agency approved 25 utility-scale solar projects from 2010 to 2012 and has 70 applications pending.[69]

FS has not approved any special use authorizations for solar projects to date, but in 2012 FS approved the first utility-scale wind power facility special use authorization. Implementation of the project to construct and operate a 15-turbine facility on the Green Mountain National Forest is pending the outcome of ongoing litigation.[70]

Woody Biomass

Removing woody biomass[71] from federal lands for energy production has received special attention because of its potential widespread availability. Biomass may serve as a renewable feedstock for energy production, and in addition, proponents assert that removing or reducing the amount of biomass density on National Forest System and BLM lands also provides landscape benefits such as improved forest resiliency and reduced risk of catastrophic wildfires. Opponents, however, are concerned that incentives to use wood and wood waste might increase land disturbances on federal lands (e.g., some of the biomass may be located in areas that are not easily accessible), and they are concerned about related wildlife, landscape, and ecosystem impacts. Other issues include the role of the federal government in developing and supporting emerging markets for woody biomass energy production, and whether to include biomass removed from federal lands in the Renewable Fuel Standard.[72]

Administration efforts to promote and implement woody biomass energy production have focused on developing policy principles, research and development, infrastructure needs, and capacity building. [73] FS and BLM both award woody biomass utilization research grants through EPAct05.[74] Programs such as stewardship contracting and the collaborative forest landscape restoration program authorize both agencies to implement woody biomass utilization projects.

CRS Product

CRS Report R40529, Biomass: Comparison of Definitions in Legislation, by Kelsi Bracmort.

Locatable Minerals

Locatable minerals include both metallic minerals (e.g., gold, silver, copper), nonmetallic minerals (e.g., mica, gypsum) and other minerals generally found in the subsurface.[75] Developing these minerals on federal lands is guided by the General Mining Law of 1872. The law, largely unchanged since 1872, grants free access to individuals and corporations to prospect for minerals in open public domain lands, and allows them, upon making a discovery, to stake (or "locate") a claim on the deposit. A claim gives the holder the right to develop the minerals and apply for a patent to obtain full title of the land and minerals. Congress is considering whether and how to reform the law, including how to capture the value of the federal resources and how to balance mineral development with competing resource values. Another issue is the lack of direct authority for environmental protection under the statute and how to address cleaning up abandoned hardrock mines. In addition, Congress has imposed a moratorium on mining claim patents in the annual Interior appropriations laws since FY1995, but has not restricted the right to stake claims or extract minerals.

The mining industry supports the claim-patent system, which offers the right to enter federal lands and freely prospect for and develop minerals. Critics consider the claim-patent system a giveaway of publicly owned resources because royalty payments are not required and the amounts paid to maintain a claim and to obtain a patent are small. New mining claim location and annual claim maintenance fees are currently $34 and $140 per claim, respectively.[76]

The Obama Administration has proposed to place most hardrock minerals produced on public lands into a leasing system, including a 5% "gross proceeds" royalty on the value of production.[77] The proposal also includes a fee on the volume of material extracted by hardrock mining on all U.S. lands to raise revenues for abandoned hardrock mine reclamation efforts.[78]

CRS Product

CRS Report RL33908, Mining on Federal Lands: Hardrock Minerals, by Marc Humphries.

RANGE MANAGEMENT

Livestock Grazing

Management of federal rangelands, particularly by the BLM and FS, presents an array of policy matters for Congress. Several issues pertain to livestock grazing. For instance, there is debate about the appropriate fee that should be charged for grazing private livestock on BLM and FS lands, including what criteria should prevail in setting the fee. Today, fees are charged under a formula established by law in 1978, then continued indefinitely through an executive order issued by President Reagan in 1986.[79] The BLM and FS are charging a grazing fee of $1.35 per animal unit month (AUM)[80] on about 139 million and 78 million acres of land respectively. This is the minimum fee established under current law. Generally, livestock producers who use federal lands want to keep fees low to sustain ranching and rural economies, while conservation groups and others seek increased fees to recover program costs or approximate market value.

The BLM and FS issue permits and/or leases to ranchers that specify the terms and conditions for grazing on agency lands. Permits and leases generally cover a 10-year period, and may be renewed. Further, expired permits and leases may be automatically renewed through FY2015 while the agencies process a backlog of permits and leases needing evaluation.[81] Questions for Congress have included whether to continue to automatically renew expiring permits/leases, extend the permit/lease length (e.g., to 20 years), and exclude the requirement for environmental analysis if current levels of grazing would continue under the renewal.

The effect of livestock grazing on rangelands has been part of a debate on the health and productivity of rangelands. Due to environmental concerns, some recent proposals would restrict or eliminate grazing, for instance, through voluntary retirement of permits and leases and subsequent closure of the allotments to grazing. These efforts are opposed by those who support ranching on the affected lands for not only environmental but lifestyle and economic reasons. Another focus of the discussion on range health and productivity is the spread of invasive and noxious weeds. (See "Invasive Species" section below.)

Wild Horses and Burros

There is continued congressional interest in management of wild horses and burros, which are protected on BLM and FS lands under the Wild Free-Roaming Horses and Burros Act of 1971.[82]

Under the act, the agencies inventory horse and burro populations on their lands to determine appropriate management levels (AMLs). While the agencies are authorized to remove animals exceeding the range's carrying capacity, currently both the BLM and FS have populations exceeding their national AMLs. Specifically, the FS estimates AML at 2,400 wild horses and burros, and population on its lands at about 5,500. BLM estimates AML at 26,677 wild horses and burros, and population at 40,605. Off the range, BLM provides funds to care for approximately 49,591 additional wild horses and burros in short-term corrals and long-term (pasture) holding facilities.

The agencies use a variety of methods to meet AML, including programs to adopt and sell animals; care for animals in holding; administer fertility control; and, most recently, establish ecosanctuaries. Questions for Congress include the sufficiency of these authorities for managing wild horses and burros. Another controversial question is whether the agencies should humanely destroy excess animals, as required under law, or whether Congress should continue to prohibit funds from being used to slaughter healthy animals. Additional issues center on the costs of management, particularly the relatively high cost of caring for animals in holding. Also, some recent proposals have focused on options for keeping animals on the range, such as by expanding areas for herds and changing the method for determining AML.

CRS Products

CRS Report RS21232, *Grazing Fees: Overview and Issues*, by Carol Hardy Vincent.

CRS Report RL34690, *Wild Horses and Burros: Issues and Proposals*, by Carol Hardy Vincent.

Recreation

The growing and diverse nature of recreation on federal lands and waters has increased the challenge of balancing different types of recreation with each other and with other land uses. At issue are questions of access to recreational opportunities, regulation of activities,—for example, through zoning or usage fees—impacts on natural and cultural resources, and the extent of motorized versus nonmotorized use.

One issue is how—or whether—fees should be collected for recreational activities on federal lands. The Federal Lands Recreation Enhancement Act (P.L. 108-447) established a recreation fee program for five federal agencies—the FLMAs and the Bureau of Reclamation. The program was set to expire in 2014, but was extended until December 8, 2015, by P.L. 113-46. Congress faces the issue of whether to let the program expire after that date, or whether to further extend it or make it permanent, as well as issues regarding the program's structure. The current program provides for various kinds of fees, specifies criteria for determining them, and establishes a national recreation pass. Agencies can use collections without further appropriation. Most of the money is for improvements at the collecting site, such as maintenance and capital improvement projects. Supporters of the program contend that it allows fees to be charged only in appropriate circumstances, sets fair and similar fees among agencies, keeps most fees on-site for improvements that visitors desire, and provides for public involvement. Among critics, some oppose recreation fees in general; others find fault with the current program, asserting, for example, that fees are appropriate for fewer agencies or types of lands, that the fee structure should be simplified and funds obligated more quickly, or that the program should ensure that most fees are used to reduce agency maintenance backlogs.

Another contentious issue is the use of off-highway vehicles (OHVs)—all-terrain vehicles, snowmobiles, personal watercraft, and others—on federal lands and waters. OHVs are a popular recreational use on BLM and FS land, while the NPS and FWS have fewer lands allowing them. OHV supporters contend that the vehicles facilitate visitor access to hard-to-reach natural areas and bring economic benefits to communities serving riders. Critics raise concerns about potential damage to wildlife habitat and ecosystems and disturbance of nonmotorized recreation. Recent Congresses have explored broad questions of OHV access to federal lands and agency management of motorized recreation in the context of oversight hearings, but legislation has largely been unit-specific, focused on OHVs at individual parks, forests, conservation areas, and other federal sites.

Access to opportunities on federal lands for hunting, fishing, and recreational shooting (e.g., at shooting ranges) is also an issue for Congress. Hunting and fishing are allowed on the majority of federal lands, but some believe they are unnecessarily restricted by agency planning processes. Others question whether opening more lands to hunting, fishing, and recreational shooting is fully consistent with good game management, public safety, other recreational uses, resource management, and the statutory purposes of the lands. In the 113th Congress, a number of bills seek to expand access to hunting, fishing, and recreational shooting, for example, by ensuring that a certain amount of LWCF funding would be used for additional physical access to hunting and fishing areas (e.g., through acquisition of lands or rights of way); by changing federal land management policies to open more land to hunting, fishing, and recreational shooting; or by giving those activities a higher priority in land management. Congress may consider which agencies' lands would be affected by such measures; whether land management and planning processes need to be changed to achieve access goals; and whether and how areas designated as wilderness would be affected.

CRS Products

CRS Report RL33730, Recreation Fees Under the Federal Lands Recreation Enhancement Act, by Carol Hardy Vincent.

CRS Report R42920, Motorized Recreation on Bureau of Land Management and Forest Service Lands, by Carol Hardy Vincent and Katie Hoover.

CRS Report R42955, Motorized Recreation on National Park Service Lands, by Laura B. Comay et al.

SPECIAL LAND DESIGNATIONS

In addition to the land protection systems administered by the individual agencies, Congress has created three cross-cutting special systems of federal lands to preserve or emphasize particular values or resources, or to protect the natural conditions for biological, recreation, or scenic purposes. These systems are the congressionally designated National Wilderness Preservation System, National Wild and Scenic Rivers System, and National Trails System. The units of these systems can be on one or more agency's lands, and the agencies manage them within parameters set in statute.

Congress and the Administration also establish other designations on federal lands, such as individual special management areas within the National Forest System. While many of the designations are unique, some have been more commonly applied, such as a national recreation area, national scenic area, or a national monument. The extent to which Congress and the Administration should expand special systems and establish other special designations on federal lands, and the types, locations, and management of such designations, continues to be controversial.

Congress has also established 49 national heritage areas (NHAs). NHA designations commemorate, conserve, or promote areas that include important natural, scenic, historic, cultural, and recreational resources. NHAs are partnerships among the NPS, states, and local communities, where the NPS supports state and local conservation through federal recognition, seed money, and technical assistance. NHAs are not part of the National Park System, where lands are federally owned and managed. Rather, lands within heritage areas typically remain in state, local, or private ownership or a combination thereof. Heritage areas have been supported as protecting lands and traditions and promoting tourism and community revitalization, but opposed as potentially burdensome, costly, or leading to federal control over nonfederal lands. Among other issues, Congress has debated whether to establish a system of NHAs, provide criteria for their designation, standards for their management, and limits on federal support.

CRS Products

CRS Report RL33462, *Heritage Areas: Background, Proposals, and Current Issues*, by Carol Hardy Vincent and Laura B. Comay.

CRS Report R41285, *Congressionally Designated Special Management Areas in the National Forest System*, by Katie Hoover.

Wilderness and Roadless Areas

In 1964, the Wilderness Act created the National Wilderness Preservation System, with statutory protections that emphasize preserving areas in their natural state. Units of the system only can be designated by Congress. Many bills to designate wilderness areas have been introduced in each Congress. The 112th Congress was the first Congress since 1964 that did not add to the wilderness system. As of January 2014, there are 759 wilderness areas, totaling nearly 110 million acres in 44 states, and managed by all four of the FLMAs. A wilderness designation generally prohibits commercial activities, motorized access, and human infrastructure from wilderness areas, subject to valid existing rights. Advocates propose wilderness designations to preserve the generally undeveloped conditions of the areas. Opponents see such designations as preventing certain uses and potential economic development in rural areas where such opportunities are relatively limited.

Designation of new wilderness areas can be controversial, and questions persist over the management of areas being considered for wilderness designation. In the FS, lands that could be considered for wilderness designation may be part of the "inventoried roadless areas". The characteristics of inventoried roadless areas in the National Forest System. Over a decade of litigation followed, with the Clinton Administration rule being enjoined twice, and the Bush Administration promulgating a rule that also was enjoined. The courts deciding the cases upheld the Clinton Administration rule, and in October, 2012, the Supreme Court refused to review the issue.

Questions also persist over BLM wilderness study areas (WSAs). WSAs are the areas BLM studied as potential wilderness, and BLM is required by FLPMA to protect their wilderness characteristics of "until Congress determines otherwise." This has raised legal questions, including whether release language is needed to allow multiple use management of WSAs not designated as wilderness. Congress has designated some WSAs as wilderness, and generally in the same statutes, Congress has released BLM from the requirement to protect the wilderness characteristics of certain other areas. However, release language in BLM wilderness statutes has generally been more controversial than for national forest areas.

CRS Products

CRS Report RL31447, *Wilderness: Overview and Statistics*, by Katie Hoover.

CRS Report R41649, *Wilderness Laws: Statutory Provisions and Prohibited and Permitted Uses*, by Kristina Alexander and Katie Hoover.

CRS Report R41610, *Wilderness: Legislation and Issues in the 113th Congress*, by Katie Hoover, Kristina Alexander, and Sandra L. Johnson.

CRS Report RL30647, *National Forest System (NFS) Roadless Area Initiatives*, by Kristina Alexander.

The National Wild and Scenic Rivers System and the National Trails System

The Wild and Scenic Rivers Act of 1968[83] created the National Wild and Scenic Rivers System. The act established a policy of preserving designated free-flowing rivers for the benefit and enjoyment of present and future generations. River units designated as part of the system are classified and administered as wild, scenic, or recreational rivers, based on the condition of the river, the amount of development in the river or on the shorelines, and the degree of accessibility by road or trail at the time of designation. Typically, rivers are added to the system by an act of Congress, but they may also be added by state nomination with the approval of the Secretary of the Interior. Congress initially designated 789 miles of eight rivers as part of the system in 1968. As of January 2014, there are 203 river units with 12,602 miles in 39 states and Puerto Rico, administered by all four of the FLMAs, or by state, local, or tribal governments.

Designation and management of lands within river corridors has been controversial in some cases. Issues include concerns about private property rights and water rights within designated river corridors. Controversies have arisen over state or federal projects prohibited within a corridor, such as construction of major highway crossings, bridges, or other activities that might affect the flow or character of the designated river segment. The extent of local input in developing river management plans is another recurring issue.

The National Trails System Act of 1968[84] created the National Trails System and authorized a national system of trails—across federal and nonfederal lands—to provide additional outdoor recreation opportunities and to promote the preservation of access to the outdoor areas and historic resources of the nation. The 1968 act established the Appalachian National Scenic Trail, stretching 2,158 miles from Maine to Georgia, and the Pacific Crest National Scenic Trail, covering 2,638 miles from Canada to Mexico through Washington, Oregon, and California. The system today includes 30 national trails (11 national scenic trails and 19 national historic trails), 1,225 national recreation trails, and 6 connecting-and-side trails. The system covers more than 67,000 miles and can be found in all 50 states, the District of Columbia, and Puerto Rico. National trails are administered by the FS, NPS, and BLM, in cooperation with appropriate state and local authorities. Most recreation uses are permitted, as are other uses or facilities that do not substantially interfere with the nature and purposes of the trail. However, motorized vehicles are generally prohibited on system trails.

Protection of national scenic and historic trails has sometimes proven challenging. Among other issues, land acquisition has sometimes been controversial. P.L. 111-11 gave federal land management agencies the authority to purchase land from willing sellers for a number of trails that had previously lacked such authority. Other issues have arisen around trail administration, involving partnerships between the federal government and volunteer nonprofit trail groups, as well as states and localities. Funding for the system is an ongoing concern. National scenic and historic trails primarily receive funding through the FLMAs that administer them, while national recreation trails receive much of their federal funding through transportation legislation. Additionally, new types of trails have occasionally been proposed for the system, such as "national discovery trails," which would be interstate trails connecting representative examples of metropolitan, urban, rural, and backcountry regions.[85]

CRS Products:

CRS Report R42614, The National Wild and Scenic Rivers System: A Brief Overview, by Sandra

L. Johnson and Laura B. Comay.

CRS Report R41081, The Wild and Scenic Rivers Act (WSRA): Protections, Federal Water Rights, and Development Restrictions, by Cynthia Brougher.

National Monuments and the Antiquities Act

The Antiquities Act of 1906[86] authorizes the President to proclaim national monuments on federal lands that contain historic landmarks, historic and prehistoric structures, or other objects of natural, historic, or scientific interest. The President is to reserve "the smallest area compatible with the proper care and management of the objects to be protected."[87] Sixteen of the 19 Presidents since 1906 have used this authority to proclaim a total of 137 monuments, including nine proclaimed by President Obama. Congress has modified many of these proclamations, has abolished some monuments, and has created monuments under its own authority.

Presidential establishment of monuments sometimes has been contentious. For instance, Congress limited the President's authority by requiring congressional authorization for extensions or establishment of monuments in Wyoming,[88] and by making withdrawals in Alaska exceeding 5,000 acres subject to congressional approval.[89] Currently, issues include the size of the areas and types of resources protected; the effects of monument designation on land uses; the level and types of threats to the areas; the inclusion of nonfederal lands within monument boundaries; the act's limited transparency process compared with the public participation and environmental review aspects of other laws; and the agency managing the monument.

Opponents have sought to revoke or impose restrictions on the President's authority to proclaim monuments. For instance, among the bills considered in recent Congresses were those that sought to block monuments from being declared in particular states; limit the size or duration of withdrawals; require the approval of Congress, the pertinent state legislature, or the pertinent governor before a monument could be proclaimed; or promote presidential creation of monuments in accordance with certain federal land management and environmental laws. Measures also were introduced to change land uses within monuments and to alter monument boundaries.

Monument supporters favor the Antiquities Act in its present form, asserting that the courts have upheld monument designations and that many past designations that initially were controversial have come to be supported. They note that Presidents of both parties have used the authority for over a century, and defend the President's authority to act promptly to protect valuable resources on federal lands that may be vulnerable to looting, vandalism, commercial development, and other permanent changes. They further contend that large segments of the public support land protection, such as through monument designations, for the recreational, preservation, and economic benefits that such designations can bring.

CRS Product

CRS Report R41330, *National Monuments and the Antiquities Act*, by Carol Hardy Vincent and Kristina Alexander.

Species Management

Each federal land agency has a responsibility to manage the plant and animal resources under its purview. An agency's authority or duty may be based on widely applicable statutes such as the Endangered Species Act, the Migratory Bird Treaty Act, or the Fish and Wildlife Coordination Act. But the agencies considered in this report also have more specific authorities in their own organic acts or in site-specific legislation.

In the case of the National Wildlife Refuge System, the conservation of plants and animals is the mission of the system, and other uses are allowed to the extent they are compatible with that mission.[90] While most refuges are open for public enjoyment, in some cases (such as island seabird colonies), the result may be a refuge that is closed to visitors. For the National Park System, resource conservation (including wildlife resources) is half of the Park Service's dual mission, shared with the other goal of public enjoyment. The missions of FS and BLM are multiple use, with species management being only one of several agency responsibilities.

The federal land management agencies do not exercise their wildlife authorities alone. Federal agencies share management of their wildlife resources with state agencies. For example, where game species are found on federal land and hunting is not expressly forbidden on that land, federal agencies work with states on wildlife censuses, and require appropriate state licenses to hunt on the federal lands. And the agencies often cooperate with states to enhance wildlife habitat to the benefit of both jurisdictions.

The four land management agencies do not maintain data on how many acres of land are currently open to hunting, fishing, and/or recreational shooting.[91] However, both BLM and the Forest Service estimate that more than 95% of their lands are currently open to these activities.[92] Among the FWS's 594 wildlife refuges and waterfowl production areas, more than 360 are open to some form of hunting, and more than 300 units offer fishing opportunities.[93] As of February 2014, hunting was permitted in 61 of the 401 NPS units, and fishing in 200 units.[94]

Congress considers species management issues such as how to balance land and resources use, when the protection of endangered and threatened species force the recognition of trade-offs among user groups. These conflicts are usually regional over resources such as surface or ground water, timber, or shorelines, to name a few.

Endangered Species

The protection of endangered and threatened species—under the 1973 Endangered Species Act (ESA)[95]—are controversial, in part, because dwindling species are often harbingers of resource scarcity. Under the ESA, all federal agencies must "utilize their authorities in furtherance of the purposes of this Act by carrying out programs for the conservation of endangered species and threatened species listed pursuant to ... this Act."[96] As a result, the federal land agencies specifically must consider listed species in their land management plans, timber sales, energy or mineral leasing plans, and all other relevant aspects of their activities. They must consult with FWS (or NMFS, for most marine species and anadromous fish such as salmon) about those effects. The majority of these consultations result in little or no change in the actions of the land managers. But some result in major controversies over the appropriate balance of land and resource use with protection of endangered and threatened species, often with some user groups allied with the listed species.

The ESA may become a focus of debate, particularly where conservation of a species signals conflict over resources in various habitats. These species include sage grouse (energy and other resources in sage brush habitat) and polar bears (energy development in northern Alaska), among others. Conflicts arise once a species is listed, because legal tools, including penalties and citizen suits, are available to aid species recovery and protect habitat. Use of these tools, or the failure to use them, has led to conflict.[97] Proposals resulting from such conflicts include granting greater authority to states over whether a species may be listed, granting priority for water projects over species recovery, and limiting the ability of citizens groups to petition for listing new species. The House Committee on Natural Resources has explored these issues in several hearings in the 113th Congress.

CRS Products

CRS Report R42945, The Endangered Species Act (ESA) in the 113th Congress: New and Recurring Issues, by M. Lynne Corn et al.

CRS Report RL31654, The Endangered Species Act: A Primer, by M. Lynne Corn and Kristina Alexander.

CRS Report RL32992, The Endangered Species Act and "Sound Science", by M. Lynne Corn and Kristina Alexander.

Invasive Species

While habitat loss is a major factor in the loss of species, invasive species have long been considered the second most important factor.[98] Invasive species may affect some of the key resources on federal lands. For example, gypsy moths have been a pest in eastern hardwoods, including national forests and Shenandoah National Park. The newly arrived fungus causing white-nose syndrome has devastated bat populations in northeastern states including those in caves on national park and national forest lands. Rats and cats threaten seabirds on coastal refuges, and goats harm rare native plant species on park units in Hawaii. In some cases, such as white-nose syndrome, no method of control is yet known, and current work is confined to research and prevention.[99] In other cases, such as the vegetation damage caused by non-native horses and burros, some control methods are considered inhumane, and others are considered expensive. In general, funding for detection, prevention, and control of invasive species on federal lands (and elsewhere) has been an issue. Several bills introduced in the 113th Congress address invasive species management on federal lands.

CRS Product

CRS Report R43258, Invasive Species: Major Laws and the Role of Selected Federal Agencies, by M. Lynne Corn and Renée Johnson.

WILDFIRE MANAGEMENT

Wildfire is a concern because it can lead to loss of human life, damage communities and timber resources,[100] and impact soils, watersheds, water quality, and wildlife. Management of wildfire— an unplanned and unwanted fire—includes preparedness, suppression, fuel reduction, site rehabilitation, and more.[101] More than 4.3 million acres burned in 2013 due to wildfire. This was less than half of the 9.3 million acres that burned in 2012.[102]

Wildfire management has been a responsibility of the federal government for over a century. The Forest Service and the DOI have overseen wildfire management, with the FS receiving approximately two-thirds of federal funding.[103] Although wildfires can occur on federal, state, or private lands, some 95% of the funding is used to protect federal lands. Wildfire management funding over the last ten years has ranged from $2.6 billion in FY2012 to $4.5 billion in FY2008.[104]

Congressional activity regarding wildfire management typically peaks during the fire season, and during the early part of the budget process.[105] Wildfire management legislative issues for Congress include oversight of the agencies' fire management activities and other wildland management practices that have altered fuel loads over time; consideration of programs and processes for reducing fuel loads;[106] rising wildfire suppression costs; and federal roles and responsibilities for wildfire protection and damages, including supplemental appropriations to deal with these issues.[107] Another issue is the impact of the expanding wildland-urban interface (WUI) which has increased the wildfire threat to people and houses. Approximately 10% of all land within the lower 48 states is classified as WUI, with a significant concentration along the East Coast, although western states have the highest proportions of homes and structures in the WUI.[108]

There is also congressional interest in FS air tanker readiness and efficacy,[109] specifically the planning for aviation resources given wildfire projections, the number and age of available air tanker units, and the contract process to place the units in service. FS aviation assessments conclude that additional resources are needed, but differ on the type, quantity, and cost of these resources.[110] In 2013, FS awarded contracts with five companies to supply the agency with new air tankers over the next five years.[111] Additionally, the National Defense Authorization Act for Fiscal Year 2014 authorizes the Department of Defense and the Department of Homeland Security to transfer aircraft to the Forest Service for wildfire suppression.[112]

CRS Products

CRS Report RL33990, Federal Funding for Wildfire Control and Management, by Kelsi Bracmort.

CRS Report RL30755, Forest Fire/Wildfire Protection, by Kelsi Bracmort.

CRS Report RS21880, Wildfire Protection in the Wildland-Urban Interface, by Kelsi Bracmort.

CRS Report R40811, *Wildfire Fuels and Fuel Reduction*, by Kelsi Bracmort.

CRS Report RL34517, *Wildfire Damages to Homes and Resources: Understanding Causes and Reducing Losses*, by Kelsi Bracmort.

CRS Report R41858, *Federal Assistance for Wildfire Response and Recovery*, by Kelsi Bracmort.

End Notes

[1] For a comprehensive listing of CRS products on federal land issues, see CRS Issues Before Congress, Energy, Environment, and Resources: Federal Lands at http://www.crs.gov/pages/subissue.aspx?cliid=314&parentid=2522& preview=False.

[2] For more information, see CRS Report R42346, Federal Land Ownership: Overview and Data.

[3] Territorial acreage is also included in the figures.

[4] This report focuses on federal land managed by the four major FMLAs and the Bureau of Ocean and Energy Management. Issues related to land management by other agencies, such as the Department of Defense, are covered in other CRS products.

[5] For more information, see CRS Report RL34267, Federal Land Ownership: Constitutional Authority and the History of Acquisition, Disposal, and Retention.

[6] The Department of Defense administers 19.4 million acres of federal land in the United States, and numerous other federal agencies—the U.S. Postal Service, the National Aeronautics and Space Administration, the Department of Energy, and many more—administer the remaining surface federal lands. Throughout the report, the term land management may include submerged land management where appropriate.

[7] P.L. 86-517; 16 U.S.C. §§ 528-531.

[8] The Wilderness Act of 1964 (P.L. 88-577; 16. U.S.C. §§1131-1136) established wilderness as a management responsibility for all of the federal land management agencies.

[9] P.L. 93-378; 16 U.S.C. §§1600, et seq.

[10] P.L. 94-588, 16 U.S.C. §§1600, et seq.

[11] These two agencies were the Grazing Service, established in 1934 to administer grazing on public rangelands, and the General Land Office, established in 1812 to oversee the disposal of the federal lands. For more information, see Paul W. Gates, History of Public Land Law Development, written for the Public Land Law Review Commission (Washington, DC: GPO, Nov. 1968), pp. 610-622.

[12] P.L. 94-579; 43 U.S.C. §§ 1701, et seq.

[13] This total excludes federal lands for which the FWS has secondary jurisdiction (another federal agency has primary jurisdiction, and the lands are counted with that agency) and nonfederal lands administered under agreements, easements, and leases. It does include the Hanford Reach National Monument (WA; 32,965 acres), which is administered by the FWS but is not part of the National Wildlife Refuge System.

[14] See "Special Marine Designations" section in this report for more information on marine national monuments.

[15] Act of August 25, 1916; 16 U.S.C. §§1-4.

[16] For a discussion of the different park titles, see CRS Report R41816, National Park System: What Do the Different Park Titles Signify?, by Laura B. Comay.

[17] 54.7 million acres, 65% of the NPS total.

[18] Order No. 3299, issued by Former Secretary of the Interior Ken Salazar issued on May 19, 2010.

[19] The Minerals Management Service (MMS) was established in 1982 after congressional committees held a number of hearings in 1981 documenting persistent problems with management of offshore energy programs. United States Commission on Fiscal Accountability of the Nation's Energy Resources, Fiscal Accountability of the Nation's Energy Resources (Washington, GPO, 1982).

[20] 43 U.S.C. §1344. The current Five Year Program went into effect August 27, 2012, and is expected to remain in effect until 2017. 77 Federal Register 40080 (July 6, 2012).

[21] P.L. 109-58, § 388(a).

[22] P.L. 90-401 and P.L. 94-422, respectively. Other OCS revenues are deposited in various accounts designated for states, other programs, and the General Treasury.

[23] 43 U.S.C. § 1331 et. seq. Generally, the OCS begins 3-9 nautical miles from shore (depending on the state) and extends 200 nautical miles outward, or farther if the continental shelf extends beyond 200 miles. The United States declared its exclusive economic zone (EEZ) in Presidential Proclamation No. 5030, 48 Federal Register 10605 (March 14, 1983); see 43 U.S.C. § 1331(a). Federal jurisdiction can be subject to principles of international law. After 1978, the OCSLA statutory framework incorporated certain requirements of the National Environmental Policy Act (NEPA, 42 U.S.C. § 4321).

[24] Not all of these acres contain energy resources.

[25] Each agency emphasizes a different mission. BSEE is responsible for safety permitting and environmental enforcement; and ONRR for collecting, auditing, and disbursing public revenues from offshore projects.

[26] 16 U.S.C. § 715 et seq. The Migratory Bird Conservation Act permanently authorized and appropriated a fund supported through the sale of hunting and conservation stamps, import duties on arms and ammunition, and a portion of certain refuge entrance fees.

[27] For more information on agency appropriations, see CRS Report R43142, Interior, Environment, and Related Agencies: FY2013 and FY2014 Appropriations, by Carol Hardy Vincent, or see CRS Issues Before Congress, Interior, Environment, and Related Agencies' Appropriations at http://www.crs.gov/pages/subissue.aspx?cliid=2346&parentid= 73& preview=False.

[28] However, monies provided to the state grant program under §105, Division C, P.L. 109-432 are permanently appropriated.

[29] These figures are estimated through FY2014.

[30] This definition is taken from the Statement of Federal Financial Accounting Standards No. 6, p. 31, available on the website of the Federal Accounting Standards Advisory Board at http://www.fasab.gov/pdffiles/sffas-6.pdf.

[31] The FY2012 estimate is the most recent readily available at publication of this report.

[32] This report does not address the causes of multi-decadal climate change. For more discussion of climate change science, see National Research Council, Advancing the Science of Climate Change, Washington DC, 2010. See also CRS Report R43229, Climate Change Science: Key Points, by Jane A. Leggett.

[33] Gregory T. Pederson, Stephen T. Gray, and Daniel B. Fagre, Long-Duration Drought Variability and Impacts on Ecosystem Services: A Case Study from Glacier National Park, Montana, U.S. Geologic Survey, Earth Interactions, Volume 10, Paper 4., January 2006, http://www.ncdc.noaa.gov/paleo/pubs/pederson2006/pederson2006.html.

[34] Executive Office of the President, The President's Climate Action Plan, June 2013, http://www.whitehouse.gov/sites/ default/files/image/president27sclimateactionplan.pdf.

[35] Executive Order 13514, "Federal Leadership in Environmental, Energy, and Economic Performance" (Washington: GPO, 2009).

[36] P.L. 91-190, 42 U.S.C. § 4321. Council on Environmental Quality, Draft Guidance for Greenhouse Gas Emissions and Climate Change Impacts, February 18, 2010, http://www. whitehouse.gov/administration/eop/ceq/initiatives/nepa/ ghg-guidance.

[37] GAO, Climate Change: Future Federal Adaptation Efforts Could Better Support Local Infrastructure Decision Makers, GAO-13-242, April 12, 2013, http://www.gao.gov/ products/gao-13-242.

[38] K. M. Archie et al., "Climate Change and Western Public Lands: A Survey of U.S. Federal Land Managers on the Status of Adaptation Efforts," Ecology and Society, vol. 17, no. 4 (2012).

[39] The Outer Continental Shelf Lands Act (OCSLA, 43 U.S.C. §1331 et. seq.) and the National Environmental Policy Act (NEPA, 42 U.S.C. § 4321).

[40] The drilling debate is a combination of several discrete debates about oil and gas leasing activity in federal waters. Congress addresses multiple issues related to access (state-federal consultations about revenue sharing, adequacy of environmental reviews, timetables for drilling permitting, operational safety, receipts and disbursements, research).

[41] P.L. 109-58. For more information about deployment of renewable energy projects, see http://www.boem.gov/Renewable-Energy-Program/Smart-from-the-Start/Index.aspx.

Estimates of OCS energy resources are available from a variety of sources, including BOEM, the Energy Information Administration, and industry sources. Due to the maturity of the offshore oil and gas sector, information supporting oil and gas reserve and resource estimates is often more robust than information about renewable resources. For a complete analysis of OCS resources, see CRS Report R40645, U.S. Offshore Oil and Gas Resources: Prospects and Processes, by Marc Humphries and Robert Pirog.

[42] The first site proposed for an offshore wind farm is off the coast of Massachusetts—the so-called "Cape Wind" project, comprising approximately 46 square miles in Nantucket Sound. See EIA Annual Energy Outlook 2012, at http://www.eia.gov/oiaf/aeo/tablebrowser/#release=AEO2013ER&subject=0-AEO2013ER&table=16-AEO2013ER&region=0-0&cases=early2013-d102312a, or Table 16 at http://www.eia.gov/forecasts/aeo/er/tables_ref.cfm.

[43] 43 U.S.C. §1337(p).

[44] 43 U.S.C. §1344. The most recent Five-Year Oil and Gas Leasing Program was approved on August 27, 2012, and covers a period from 2012 through 2017.

[45] In 2011, BOEM conveyed 181 new leases to qualified companies operating in the Gulf of Mexico as part of issuing new oil and gas leases. In addition, BOEM approved 1,342 applications from companies owning existing leases requesting BOEM change the record of lease ownership to another company. BOEM written communication to CRS October 9, 2012. BOEM approved the following lease assignments during 2011: 358 applications for assignments involving 100% ownership interest in a lease and 984 applications for assignments involving less than 100% ownership interest in a lease.

[46] For more information about this process, see CRS Report RL33404, Offshore Oil and Gas Development: Legal Framework, by Adam Vann.

[47] National Marine Sanctuaries Act, 16 U.S.C. 1431 et seq.

[48] One of the purposes and policies of the National Marine Sanctuaries Act (NMSA) is to "cooperate globally." In other words, Congress recognized a need to work outside sanctuaries' boundaries to fully comply with the primary mandate to protect sanctuary resources.

[49] Budget Justifications, Bureau of Land Management, FY2013, p. VIII-107.

[50] 30 U.S.C. §181.

[51] Exceptions include most BLM and FS lands classified as wilderness, lands incorporated in cities and towns, and lands that have otherwise been administratively or statutorily withdrawn from entry.

[52] P.L. 109-58.

[53] For further information, see CRS Report R40806, Energy Projects on Federal Lands: Leasing and Authorization, by Adam Vann.

[54] U.S. Departments of the Interior, of Agriculture, and of Energy, Inventory of Onshore Federal Oil and Natural Gas Resources and Restrictions to Their Development (Phase III), May 2008, available on the BLM website at http://www.blm.gov/wo/st/en/prog/energy/oil_and_gas/EPCA_III.html. The availability of public lands for oil and gas leasing can be divided into three categories: lands open under standard lease terms, open to leasing with restrictions, and closed to leasing.

[55] 77 Fed. Reg. 27691, May 11, 2012, and 78 Fed. Reg. 31636, May 24, 2013.

[56] Bureau of Land Management, "Average Application for Permit to Drill (APD) Approval Timeframes: FY2005- FY2012," http://www.blm.gov/wo/st/en/prog/energy/ oil_and_gas/statistics/apd_chart.html.

[57] U.S. Department of the Interior, Bureau of Land Management, Year Two Report: Section 365 of the Energy Policy Act of 2005—Pilot Project to Improve Federal Permit Coordination (Feb. 2008).

[58] U.S. Government Accountability Office, Coal Leasing: BLM Could Enhance Appraisal Process, More Explicitly Consider Coal Exports, and Provide More Public Information, GAO-14-140, December 2013, http://www.gao.gov/ assets/660/659801.pdf.

[59] U.S. Department of the Interior, Office of Inspector General, Coal Management Program, CR-EV-BLM-0001-2012, June 11, 2013, http://www.doi.gov/oig/reports/upload/CR-EV-BLM-0001-2012Public.pdf.

[60] As of March 2013, 29 states and the District of Columbia have enforceable renewable portfolio standards, and 8 states have voluntary goals for renewable generation. U.S. Department of Energy, Database of State Incentives for Renewables & Efficiency, March 2013, http://www.dsireusa.org/documents/summarymaps/RPS_map.pdf.

[61] 30 U.S.C. §§1001-1028.

[62] BLM and Forest Service, Record of Decision and Resource Management Plan Amendments for Geothermal Leasing in the Western United States, BLM-WO-GI-09-003-1800, December 2008, http://www.blm.gov/ Geothermal_EIS.

[63] Budget Justification, BLM FY2013.

[64] 43 U.S.C. §§1761-1771.

[65] BLM, "Segregation of Lands-Renewable Energy," 78 Fed. Reg. 25204, April 30, 2013.

[66] BLM Fact Sheet, Renewable Energy and the BLM, Wind, Updated September 2013.

[67] These six states are Arizona, California, Colorado, Nevada, New Mexico, and Utah. BLM Fact Sheet, Renewable Energy and the BLM: Solar, Updated September 2013.

[68] Scott Streater, "First-ever auction of solar-zone parcels draw zero industry interest," E&E News PM, October 24, 2013, http://www.eenews.net/eenewspm/stories/1059989375/.

[69] Ibid.

[70] For more information, see the FS Deerfield Wind Energy Development Special Use Permit EIS webpage: http://data.ecosystem-management.org/nepaweb/fs-usda-pop.php?project =7838.

[71] Woody biomass is defined by FS and BLM as the trees and woody plants, including limbs, tops, needles, leaves, and other woody parts, grown in a forest, woodland, or rangeland environment that are the byproducts of forest management.

[72] For more information on the renewable fuel standard, see CRS Report R43325, The Renewable Fuel Standard: In Brief, by Kelsi Bracmort and CRS Report R40155, Renewable Fuel Standard (RFS): Overview and Issues, by Randy Schnepf and Brent D. Yacobucci.

[73] See for example, Memorandum of Understanding on Policy Principles for Woody Biomass Utilization for Restoration and Fuel Treatments in Forests, Woodlands, and Rangelands, June 2003, http://www.fs.fed.us/woodybiomass/documents/Biomass MOU_060303_final_web.pdf and Forest Service, Woody Biomass Utilization Desk Guide, September 2007, http://www.forests and rangelands.gov/Woody_ Biomass/documents/biomass_deskguide.pdf.

[74] See for example, http://www.forestsandrangelands.gov/Woody_Biomass/opportunities.shtml.

[75] Management of non-locatable minerals (e.g., sand, gravel, and stone) on federal lands is governed by the Materials Act of 1947.

[76] The fees are to be adjusted every five years based on the Consumer Price Index (30 U.S.C. 28 j (c)).

[77] Budget Justification, BLM, FY2013.

[78] Budget Justifications, BLM, FY2013.

[79] P.L. 95-514, 92 Stat. 1803; 43 U.S.C. §§1901, 1905. Executive Order 12548, 51 Fed. Reg. 5985 (February 19, 1986).

[80] BLM defines an AUM, for fee purposes, as a month's use and occupancy of the range by one animal unit, which includes one yearling, one cow and her calf, one horse, or five sheep or goats. The FS uses head-month (HD-MO) as its measurement for use and occupancy of FS lands. AUM is used in this memorandum to cover both HD-MO and AUM.

[81] P.L. 113-76, Sec. 411.

[82] 16 U.S.C. §§ 1331 et seq.

[83] P.L. 90-542, 16 U.S.C. §§1271 et seq. "87 Sixteen of the 19

[84] P.L. 90-543; 16 U.S.C. §§1241 et seq.

[85] See, for example, H.R. 3022 in the 113th Congress. Similar bills were introduced in previous Congresses.

[86] 16 U.S.C. § 431.

[87] 16 U.S.C. §431.

[88] 16 U.S.C. §431a.

[89] 16 U.S.C. §3213.

[90] National Wildlife Refuge System Administration Act of 1966 (16 U.S.C. 668dd et seq.).

[91] Personal communication between Laura Comay of CRS and NPS (Chris Powell, Senior Congressional Affairs Specialist) and BLM (Division of Legislative Affairs); Personal communication between Katie Hoover of CRS and. FS (Tony Edwards, Legislative Affairs Specialist); Personal communication between Lynne Corn of CRS and FWS (Martin Kodis, Deputy Chief, Division of Congressional and Legislative Affairs).

[92] The BLM estimate is derived from testimony in the 112th Congress on H.R. 3440, H.R. 2834, and H.R. 1444 regarding recreational shooting and hunting, and personal communication between BLM and Carol Hardy-Vincent of CRS, February 19, 2014. The FS estimate is from personal communication between Katie Hoover of CRS and Tony Edwards, FS Legislative Affairs Specialist, February 21, 2014.

[93] U.S. Fish and Wildlife Service, April 2013, http://www.fws.gov/refuges/about/pdfs/RecreationFactSheetApril2013.pdf.

[94] Personal communication between Laura Comay of CRS and Chris Powell, NPS Senior Congressional Affairs Specialist, February 21, 2014. Units may be completely open to hunting or fishing, or these activities may be permitted only in portions of the unit.

[95] P.L. 93-205, as amended; 16 U.S.C. §§1531-1543.

[96] 16 U.S.C. 1536(a).

[97] A more detailed discussion of the major provisions of ESA is provided in CRS Report RL31654, The Endangered Species Act: A Primer, by M. Lynne Corn, Kristina Alexander, and Eugene H. Buck.

[98] For example, see Randy G. Westbrooks, Invasive Plants: Changing the Landscape of America, Federal Interagency Committee for the Management of Noxious and Invasive Weeds, Washington, DC, 1998, p. 5.

[99] For an example of prevention efforts, see those at Mammoth Cave National Park, where the fungus has already been found: http://www.nps.gov/maca/whitenose.htm.

[100] For more information on wildfire damages to homes and resources, see CRS Report RL34517, Wildfire Damages to Homes and Resources: Understanding Causes and Reducing Losses, by Kelsi Bracmort.

[101] Preparedness is any activity that leads to a safe, efficient and cost-effective fire management program, as well as the range of tasks necessary to build, sustain, and improve the capability to protect against, respond to, and recover from domestic incidents. Suppression is all of the work associated with extinguishing or confining a fire. Fuel reduction is manipulation, including combustion, or removal of fuels to reduce the likelihood of ignition and/or to lessen potential damage and resistance to control. Site rehabilitation is efforts undertaken generally within three years of a wildfire to repair or improve fire damaged lands unlikely to recover to a management approved condition, or to repair or replace minor facilities damaged by fire.

[102] The acreage burned in 2012 was the third largest acreage burned annually based on historical fire statistics, which were first reported in 1960. The first and second largest fire year on record for acres burned was 2006 and 2007, respectively. National Interagency Fire Center, Current year-to-date by state (2013);http://www.nifc.gov/fireInfo/ fireInfo_stats_YTD2012.html National Interagency Fire Center, Wildland Fire Summary and Statistics Annual Report (2013), http://www.predictiveservices.nifc.gov/intelligence/ 2013_Statssumm/intro_summary13.pdf.

[103] Wildfire management is funded under the Interior, Environment and Related Agencies appropriations bill. For more information on federal funding for wildfire management, see CRS Report R43077, Wildfire Management: Federal Funding and Related Statistics, by Kelsi Bracmort, and CRS Report RL33990, Federal Funding for Wildfire Control and Management, by Kelsi Bracmort.

[104] Ibid.

[105] The fires season generally starts in mid or late summer and ends in mid or late fall. Factors such as wind, drought, precipitation events from the previous year, and more contribute to the length and severity of the fire season.

[106] For more information on options for fuel reduction, see CRS Report R40811, Wildfire Fuels and Fuel Reduction, by Kelsi Bracmort.

[107] For more information, see CRS Report RL30755, Forest Fire/Wildfire Protection, by Kelsi Bracmort.

[108] For more information, see CRS Report RS21880, Wildfire Protection in the Wildland-Urban Interface, by Kelsi Bracmort.

[109] The FS reports that the average age of air tankers still in service is more than 50 years old. USDA Forest Service, Large Airtanker Modernization Strategy, January 17, 2012http://www.fs.fed.us/fire/aviation/ airtanker_modernization_strategy.pdf.

[110] RAND Corporation, Air Attack Against Wildfires: Understanding U.S. Forest Service Requirements for Large Aircraft, 2012http://www.rand.org/pubs/monographs/MG1234.html; National Interagency Aviation Council, Interagency Aviation Strategy, July 2008; Fire Program Solutions LLC, Wildland Fire Management Aerial Application Study, USDA Forest Service, October 17, 2005; Forest Service, Federal Aerial Firefighting: Assessing Safety and Effectiveness, December 2002; USDA Forest Service, National Study of Airtankers to Support Initial Attack and Large Fire Suppression, 1995http://www.fs.fed.us/fire/publications/aviation/nats1_report.pdf.

[111] Forest Service, "U.S. Forest Service issues notice of intent to award "Next Generation" airtanker contracts," press release, May 6, 2013, http://www.fs.fed.us/news/ 2013/releases/05/next-gen-tanker.shtml.

[112] P.L. 113-66 Sec. 1098.

In: Federal Land Policy
Editor: Felicia Martin

ISBN: 978-1-63482-168-1

Chapter 2

FEDERAL LAND MANAGEMENT AGENCIES: APPROPRIATIONS AND REVENUES*

Carol Hardy Vincent, Laura B. Comay, M. Lynne Corn, Curry L. Hagerty, Katie Hoover and William J. Mallett

SUMMARY

A perennial focus for Congress is on appropriations for management of federal lands and resources. Issues include the purposes for which appropriations are used, factors influencing their distribution among states, and the extent to which appropriations are used on nonfederal lands. Congress also continues to be interested in the revenues derived from federal lands and resources. Questions relate to the amount of revenue generated on federal lands, the sources of revenue, and factors affecting the variation among states in the amount and type of revenue generated.

Approximately 95% of federal lands are managed by four agencies: the Bureau of Land Management (BLM), Fish and Wildlife Service (FWS), National Park Service (NPS), and Forest Service (FS). Their FY2013 appropriations were $2,048.1 million for BLM, $2,591.6 million for FWS, $3,305.8 million for NPS, and $5,709.8 million for FS. Of these totals, FS received the largest discretionary appropriation ($4,934.7 million) while FWS had the highest mandatory appropriation ($1,053.1

* This is an edited, reformatted and augmented version of a Congressional Research Service publication, No. R43822, dated December 10, 2014.

million). The largest discretionary appropriation for FS was for Wildland Fire Management; for the other three agencies, it was the main operations account. The agencies have many sources of mandatory appropriations, some of which are common among them and across states (e.g., recreation fees) while others are unique to one agency or allocated to one state. Another distinction concerns the portion of appropriations used on lands not managed by the agencies, ranging from little in the case of BLM to roughly two-thirds for FWS.

Revenue collections during FY2013 differed among the agencies, with \$18.9 million for FWS, \$223.6 million for FS, \$333.4 million for NPS, and \$525.0 million for BLM. Depending on the agency and state, sources of revenue might include land sales, grazing, timber, hardrock minerals, recreation, and rights of way. Influencing the allocation of appropriations among states and the amount of revenue collected in each state were the acreage of federal land; land resources, conditions, availability, uses, and impacts; demographics; fire activity; and other factors.

BLM, FWS, NPS, and FS also receive federal lands highway funds from the Federal Highway Administration. A total of \$573.8 million in highway funding for federal lands was distributed in FY2013, with almost half (\$280.6 million) going to NPS and another two-fifths (\$227.2 million) to state Programming Decisions Committees (bodies that make some project funding decisions). The remainder went to FWS (\$36.5 million), FS (\$19.8 million), and BLM (\$9.6 million). Distributions among states ranged from less than \$0.1 million to \$86.5 million.

The Payments in Lieu of Taxes program and FS Payments to States program compensate local governments for the presence of federally owned land. PILT applies to many types of federal lands, and payments are calculated under a formula. The total PILT payment in FY2013 was \$401.8 million, with state totals ranging from \$0 to \$41.4 million (for California). The FS Payments to States program—which includes Secure Rural Schools (SRS) payments—applies to counties with national forest lands and certain BLM forested lands. Payments are based on either historic or current revenue generated on the lands, and other considerations. FY2013 payments to states totaled \$312.5 million, ranging from less than \$0.1 million to \$97.1 million (for Oregon).

The Department of the Interior's Office of Natural Resources Revenue (ONRR) collects mineral leasing revenues from all federal onshore areas. Revenue is derived from many commodities, including coal, gas, hardrock minerals, oil, phosphate, sodium, and sulfur. For FY2013, ONRR reported \$4,296.9 million from federal lands in 37 states, with revenues by state of less than \$0.1 million to \$1,998.9 million (for Wyoming).

INTRODUCTION

Two perennial issues for Congress are appropriations for management of federal lands and resources, and the revenues derived from these lands and resources. The focus of legislative action has been on the four major federal land management agencies: the Bureau of Land Management (BLM), Fish and Wildlife Service (FWS), and National Park Service (NPS) in the Department of the Interior (DOI) and the Forest Service (FS) in the Department of Agriculture.[1] In determining discretionary appropriations for these agencies, Congress establishes the level of funds for diverse programs, projects, and activities. Congress also has enacted legislation to provide mandatory appropriations for varied programs and purposes. Further, these agencies receive distributions of funding from other agencies for specific purposes.

How appropriations for federal land management are used throughout the states is of continuing interest to Congress. Questions relate to the amount of each agency's appropriations used within a particular state, factors influencing the distribution of appropriations among states, the purposes for which appropriations are used, and the extent to which appropriations are used on federal versus nonfederal land in each state.

Other questions pertain to the revenues generated from federally managed lands. They include the amount of revenue generated on federal lands, the sources of revenue, and factors influencing the variation among states in the amount and type of revenue generated on federal lands.

In this context, this report provides information on appropriations and revenues related to federal lands in each state.[2] It focuses on lands managed by the BLM, FWS, NPS, and FS, as these agencies administer approximately 95% of the roughly 640 million acres of federal land.[3] In particular, this report provides state-by-state information in four areas:

- appropriations for, and revenues collected by, the four agencies,
- distributions of funds from the Federal Highway Administration (FHWA) to the four agencies for their lands,
- payments under the Payments in Lieu of Taxes (PILT) program and the Secure Rural Schools and Community Self Determination Act of 2000 (SRS), and
- mineral leasing revenues for onshore federal lands, as reported by the DOI Office of Natural Resources Revenue (ONRR).

Comprehensive data covering these areas do not exist in a single source.[4] State-by-state data for some types of information are readily available in public sources,[5] as identified in the pertinent sections below. Where this was not the case, CRS sought to obtain the information directly from the pertinent agencies.[6]

Organization of Report

The first four sections of this report pertain to appropriations for the four major land management agencies and revenues collected by those agencies.[7] The appropriations figures represent budget authority, both discretionary and mandatory. For all four agencies, discretionary appropriations are provided primarily through the annual Interior, Environment, and Related Agencies Appropriations law. The agencies have varied sources of mandatory funding under legislation originated by authorizing committees. Laws authorizing mandatory appropriations allow the agencies to spend money without further action by Congress.[8]

Appropriations figures in this report generally represent *new* budget authority for FY2013[9] and thus generally do not include appropriations carried over from prior fiscal years.[10] Figures representing total budget authority could present a different picture of agency funding for some states.[11] Figures showing obligations or expenditures[12] of funds also could differ considerably in some cases from the appropriations figures used in this report.[13] Appropriations figures in this report also reflect any supplemental funds for FY2013 and reductions under the sequester order of the President of March 1, 2013.[14]

By contrast, revenue figures throughout this report represent the actual amounts collected, because revenues are not subject to sequestration. The revenue data in the BLM, FWS, NPS, and FS sections reflect revenues collected by each agency, whether these revenues were retained by the agencies for use in the state where collected, used by the agency for other purposes, or allocated to another source (e.g., to the general fund of the Treasury). Depending on the agency, sources of revenue might include land sales, grazing, timber, recreation entrance/use, hardrock minerals, and rights of way, among others. The revenue data in these sections do not reflect the share of each agency's revenues, if any, from onshore mineral leasing. This is because these revenues are collected by the DOI Office of Natural Resources Revenue for all federal lands, as discussed below.

Distributions to the BLM, FWS, NPS, and FS from the Federal Highway Administration are shown in the fifth section of this report. The funds are from several federal lands highway programs. They are the largest allocations to the four agencies outside of the departments in which they are located (DOI and Department of Agriculture).[15]

The sixth section of this report provides information on payments under the PILT and FS Payments to States programs. These programs compensate local governments for the presence of most federally owned land. PILT applies to many types of federal land, while the FS payments apply to counties with national forest lands and certain BLM forested lands.[16]

The ONRR section of this report, presented next, reflects the mineral leasing revenues from all federal onshore areas. The revenues are derived from a variety of energy and mineral activities on federal lands, involving a wide array of commodities.[17] Finally, the **Appendix** lists the federal acreage managed by each of the four agencies, by state.

Caveats

Several caveats about interpreting the information in this report deserve note. First, this report provides statistics for only one year. While some funding amounts might be largely consistent from year to year, others might vary by different degrees. For example, congressional and presidential priorities might change, influencing funding for particular programs, projects, and activities and the location of agency spending. Also, the appropriations to agencies for wildland fire management, and their distribution among states, vary from year to year in part depending on the severity of fires. Similarly, land acquisition may occur in some states and not others in any given year. Another factor is unplanned events, such as natural or man-made disasters, as shown by the appropriation of supplemental funds for FY2013 to address the consequences of Superstorm Sandy.[18] Still other factors relate to the budgetary framework, with one example being the reduction of FY2013 appropriations under the President's sequester order of March 1, 2013.[19]

Second, figures in this report should be regarded as estimates and are not aggregated across agencies or across states, for a variety of reasons. For one, the agencies receive and allocate appropriations differently. The allocation might be by state or by other geographic area, such as by national forest (which may cross state lines) or regional office. Agencies also differ as to how they define, organize, and report data. For instance, revenue data might reflect total revenue collected by an agency or only revenues collected from activities and resources on lands the agency owns. For example, BLM data include payments from federal, state, and local governments for fire work performed on non-BLM land, but the FS data reflect revenue generated exclusively on FS lands. Another difference is how agencies reflect appropriations for operations of their headquarters or regional offices. For instance, FWS and NPS reflect headquarters appropriations with the state in which the headquarters are located, while BLM does not reflect them with any state.

An additional complication in making comparisons across agencies is whether to consider total appropriations or only those used on agency-owned lands. This is because agencies differ considerably in the extent to which they use appropriations in a state on lands other than those they own. As an illustration of this point, FWS uses about two-thirds of its appropriations on lands not managed by the agency, while virtually all of BLM appropriations are used on agency-managed lands.

There is also overlap in some of the information provided by the agencies and reported here, such as for some mandatory appropriations included in both an agency's appropriations and its revenue totals (e.g., for recreation). Further, some amounts are reflected in multiple sections of this report, as is the case for SRS monies reflected in the BLM, FS, and SRS sections. As a result of these overlaps, aggregation could lead to double counting of some monies. Additional challenges and issues associated with particular data in this report are discussed in the pertinent sections.

Third, this report does not provide information on the broader economic dimensions related to federal lands managed by the four agencies. An analysis of economic costs and benefits and other impacts is beyond the scope of this report.

Fourth, this report is not intended to make implications about these lands if they were under nonfederal ownership, such as the level of funds that might be provided for their management; the revenues that might be generated through their use; or the broader economic costs, benefits, and impacts that might occur. For example, the legal and political frameworks pertinent to management under state law may vary considerably from those that apply to the BLM, FWS, NPS, and FS.

Finally, for all categories of data, figures are provided for FY2013 as the most recent fiscal year for which data were available across categories. Throughout the report, figures generally are rounded to the closest million. Due to rounding, figures of less than $50,000 are shown as <$0.1 million. Territories are not shown in a table if they did not receive the appropriations or payments, or collect the revenues, shown in the table. Also, figures may not sum to the totals provided due to rounding.

Overview

BLM, FWS, NPS, and FS received widely varying amounts of FY2013 appropriations for federal land management, as shown in Figure 1. Each agency dispersed its appropriations differently among the states. The lands of these agencies across states also generated widely differing amounts of revenue. Influencing the allocation of appropriations among states, and the amount of revenue collected in each state, were the acreage of federal land; land resources, conditions, availability, uses, and impacts; demographics; fire activity; and other factors. Many of these factors are common among the agencies, while others apply more particularly to one or a subset of agencies. For instance, FWS appropriations used in a state are particularly affected by the number of species listed under the Endangered Species Act, entry ports for regulated wildlife, and two major state grant programs for conservation of game and sport fish (Wildlife Restoration and Sportfish Restoration).

The FY2013 appropriation to the FS ($5,709.8 million) was more than twice the appropriation to BLM ($2,048.1 million) and FWS ($2,591.6 million) and more than 40% bigger than the appropriation for NPS ($3,305.8 million). Of these totals, FS received the most in discretionary appropriations ($4,934.7 million), while FWS had the highest mandatory appropriation ($1,053.1 million). Wildland Fire Management constituted the largest portion of FS appropriations for the 12 states covered in this report (and overall). For the other three agencies, the biggest appropriation was for the main operations and management account.

The agencies have many sources of mandatory appropriations, some of which are common among them and across states (e.g., recreation). Others are unique to one agency, with the contribution for annuity benefits for U.S. Park Police being one example. Still other mandatory accounts are specific to not only one agency but one state; this is the case for BLM's appropriations for Secure Rural Schools payments, which are made to Oregon. The largest mandatory appropriations differed among the agencies: for BLM, the Helium Production Fund[20]; for FWS, state grants for conservation of game and sport fish (Wildlife Restoration and Sportfish Restoration); for NPS, recreation fees; and for FS, payments to states generally.

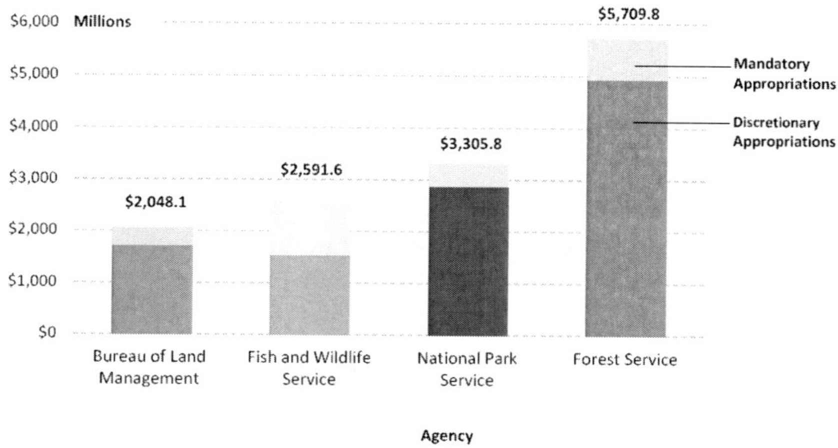

Source: Prepared by CRS with data from various sources. Figures for BLM, FWS, and NPS were derived primarily from the respective agencies. FS discretionary appropriations data are derived from detailed funding tables prepared by the House Committee on Appropriations. FS mandatory appropriations data are derived from Forest Service, *Fiscal Year 2015 Budget Justification*, at http://www.fs.fed.us/sites/default/files/media

Notes: Figures reflect total appropriations for all agencies. For details related to a particular agency, see the pertinent appropriations sections in this report.

Figure 1. Comparison of Appropriations by Agency, FY2013; (in millions of dollars).

Another distinction is in the extent to which the four agencies use appropriations on lands other than those they manage. Very little if any of BLM appropriations for most states are used on nonBLM lands. A relatively small amount of NPS and FS appropriations are used off agency lands. By contrast, roughly two-thirds of FWS appropriations are used on lands under non-FWS ownership.

Revenue collections during FY2013 were small for the FWS ($18.9 million) as compared with the other agencies. BLM's revenue collections were the largest ($525.0 million). They were more than double the FS amount ($223.6 million) and more than one-third bigger than NPS collections ($333.4 million). Depending on the agency and state, sources of revenue might include land sales, grazing, timber, hardrock minerals, recreation, and rights of way. Sales of helium were the biggest revenue source for BLM. FWS had four revenue sources of roughly the same size (from $4.0 million to $5.0 million). On NPS lands, recreation generated the most revenue ($179.5 million). While recreation also was the single largest source of revenue on FS lands ($61.4

million), revenue/collections associated with timber or salvage timber sales collectively were a larger portion of FS revenues ($129.5 million). **Figure 2** shows revenues collected by agency.

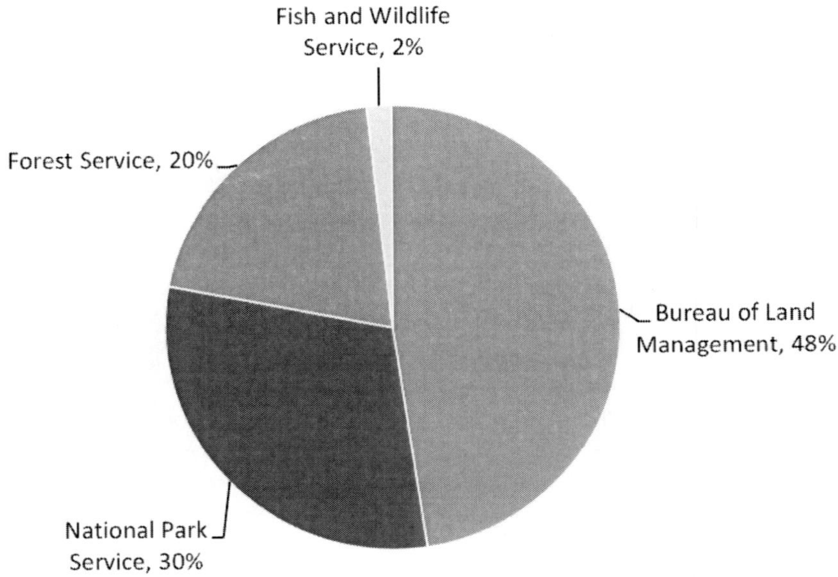

Source: Prepared by CRS with data from various sources. BLM and NPS figures were derived primarily from data from the respective agencies. FWS information was derived from U.S. Department of the Interior, Budget Justifications and Performance Information, Fiscal Year 2015, Fish and Wildlife Service, at http://www.fws.gov/budget/2014/FY2015_FWS_Greenbook-DOI31014.pdf. FS information was derived from U.S. Department of Agriculture, Forest Service, All Service Receipts (ASR), Final Forest Statement of Receipts (ASR-13-2), http://www.fs.usda.gov/Internet/FSE_DOCUMENTS/stelprd3795423.pdf.

Notes: For details related to a particular agency, see the pertinent revenue sections in this report.

Figure 2. Comparison of Revenues Collected by Agency, FY2013.

Supplementing the appropriations to BLM, FWS, NPS, and FS are allocations of funding from outside the agencies. A major allocation is from the Federal Highway Administration for federal lands highway programs. Of the total distributed in FY2013 ($573.8 million), the NPS received almost half ($280.6 million), and another two-fifths ($227.2 million) went to state Programming Decisions Committees. Smaller amounts were allocated to the

FWS ($36.5 million), FS ($19.8 million), and BLM ($9.6 million). With a distribution of $86.5 million, California received significantly more funds than any other state; the next largest distribution was $36.1 million for Montana, and only nine states received more than $20.0 million.[21] Two eastern states—Connecticut and Delaware—received the lowest distributions (less than $0.1 million). Factors affecting the distribution among states include the amount of federal lands, public road miles, recreational visitation, and federal public bridges as well as agency priorities.

The Payments in Lieu of Taxes program and FS Payments to States program compensate local governments for the presence of federally owned land. PILT applies to many types of federal lands, with payments based on county population and several other factors. Of the total PILT payment in FY2013 ($401.8 million), 17 states (and other areas) received less than $1.0 million, while 10 states received more than $20.0 million. The FS Payments to States program provided $312.5 million in FY2013 payments to counties with national forest lands and certain BLM forested lands. Payments are based on either historic or current revenue generated on the lands and other considerations. Of the 41 states that received FY2013 payments, 21 received less than $2.0 million.[22] Oregon received the highest payment—$97.1 million—about three times more than the next highest state.

From federal onshore areas, ONRR reported collecting $4,296.9 million in mineral leasing revenues during FY2013. The revenue was from different types of payments: bonuses, rents, and royalties. It derived from many energy and mineral commodities, including coal, gas, hardrock minerals, oil, phosphate, sodium, and sulfur. The FY2013 total was from federal lands in 37 states. Wyoming and New Mexico together accounted for more than two-thirds of the total, while about half the states had revenue of less than $1.0 million (including 13 states with no onshore receipts). Revenue levels not only vary widely among states but can vary considerably from year to year. Factors affecting revenues derived in each state include the amount of federal acreage, the extent of that acreage containing recoverable energy and mineral resources, weather conditions, and other circumstances.

The total funding for federal land management in a state, and total revenues derived from federal lands in a state, are difficult to ascertain with certainty for varied reasons. They include differences among agencies in how they receive and allocate appropriations and define, organize, and report data. For these and other reasons, figures in this report are not aggregated across states. Moreover, there are variations from year to year in appropriations among states and revenues derived on federal lands across states. This report provides a snapshot of one fiscal year.

BUREAU OF LAND MANAGEMENT

Appropriations

The Bureau of Land Management (BLM) estimates that appropriations for FY2013 were $2,048.1 million.[23] The majority of this funding was discretionary. Specifically, the total includes $1,714.9 million (83.7%) in discretionary appropriations and $333.1 million (16.3%) in mandatory appropriations. According to the BLM, virtually all appropriations to the agency are used for managing agency-owned lands.[24] **Table 1** and **Figure 3** provide the discretionary, mandatory, and total BLM appropriations by state.

Discretionary Appropriations

For FY2013, BLM received $1,714.9 million in discretionary appropriations through six accounts, as shown in **Table 2**. The largest account was for Management of Lands and Resources, which in FY2013 received $1,020.9 million (59.5%) of BLM's discretionary appropriation. This account funds an array of BLM programs and activities, including land resources, wildlife and fisheries, threatened and endangered species, recreation, energy and minerals, and resource planning for agency lands. The second-largest discretionary appropriation was for Wildland Fire Management.[25] This account funds fire preparedness and suppression, hazardous fuels reduction, and other programs. BLM's allocation from this department-wide account comprised $478.1 million (27.9%) of the agency's discretionary appropriations for FY2013.

The FY2013 appropriations for BLM's four other discretionary accounts were considerably smaller. Oregon and California Grant Lands received $106.0 million (6.2%) of the discretionary appropriation for managing certain timberlands in western Oregon.[26] Another $62.4 million (3.6%) was for the Working Capital Fund, a revolving fund used for purchasing supplies, equipment, facilities, and services in support of BLM programs.[27] Service Charges, Deposits, and Forfeitures provided $26.3 million (1.5%) of discretionary appropriations. The account funds administrative expenses and other costs of certain BLM actions for which the public has paid fees, such as for processing applications and authorizations for use of public lands and resources. The remaining $21.2 million (1.2%) of the discretionary appropriation was for Land Acquisition, for BLM to acquire lands or interests in land.[28]

Mandatory Appropriations

A variety of laws provide for mandatory appropriations for BLM. Of the $333.1 million provided under these laws in FY2013, the largest amount was from the Helium Production Fund—about three-fifths ($202.2 million, 60.7%) of the FY2013 mandatory appropriation. In FY2013, receipts from BLM sales of federal crude helium were deposited in the Helium Production Fund.[29] The second-largest mandatory appropriation, with $38.0 million (11.4%) of the total, was for Secure Rural Schools payments to western Oregon counties.[30] The Land and Resources Management Trust Fund, with $21.8 million (6.5%) of the mandatory appropriations, reflects donations to BLM from individuals, companies, state agencies, and others for certain activities and services. Another $17.5 million (5.3%) was from receipts from recreation fees, with $16.7 million (5.0%) from onshore mineral leasing receipts deposited in the Permit Processing Improvement Fund. Land disposals in Nevada under the Southern Nevada Public Land Management Act and livestock grazing on BLM lands (Range Improvements) generated another $10.5 million (3.2%) and $9.5 million (2.9%), respectively. The remaining $16.9 million (5.1%) of mandatory appropriations derived from several other sources. **Table 3** contains the mandatory appropriations by account.

Discussion

BLM manages its lands through 12 state offices, which in some cases administer BLM lands and onshore federal minerals in more than one state. Each of these state offices received a portion of BLM's FY2013 appropriations, as did the Office of Fire and Aviation, a national-level office. Other FY2013 appropriations were not allocated to any state office. Most of these funds, shown as "no state" in the tables, were provided to BLM headquarters in Washington, DC, for expenses that support all BLM land management and national programs.

As shown in **Table 1** and **Figure 3**, BLM state offices received widely varying amounts of FY2013 appropriations, ranging from $17.0 million for all eastern states to $299.6 million for New Mexico. The level of appropriations allocated by BLM to state offices is influenced by a number of factors. One is the amount of lands and onshore federal minerals managed by BLM, of which acreages vary widely among states.[31] Different land resources, conditions, uses, and impacts can affect the cost of land management, as can demographics. Another variable is the extent of wildfire suppression and other fire activity, which affects the allocation of funds among states for wildland fire management.

Another factor is that some programs may have no or very little activity within a state, resulting in none or a small portion of these program funds being allocated to the state. In particular, some programs are specific to one state, and some of these state-specific programs received relatively large appropriations. For example, the New Mexico state office received the largest FY2013 appropriation because BLM's sale of helium is shown as budget authority for that state.[32] Excluding the Helium Production Fund, the appropriation for New Mexico would have been about two-thirds lower—$97.4 million. As a second example, the Oregon state office received the second-largest appropriation among states ($283.4 million),[33] primarily because it received the overwhelming majority of the discretionary appropriations for Oregon and California Grant Lands and the mandatory appropriation for Secure Rural Schools.[34]

Table 1. Bureau of Land Management Appropriations by State, FY2013 (in millions of dollars)

	Discretionary Appropriations	Mandatory Appropriations	Total Appropriations
Alaska	111.9	1.1	113.0
Arizona	75.4	2.5	77.9
California	142.5	10.2	152.7
Colorado	89.0	3.5	92.4
Eastern states	17.0	<0.1	17.0
Idaho	120.6	2.6	123.3
Montana	85.3	4.3	89.6
New Mexico	88.0	211.5	299.6
Nevada	170.1	17.1	187.2
Oregon	237.8	45.7	283.4
Utah	114.9	6.0	120.9
Wyoming	96.1	6.6	102.7
Subtotal	*1,439.8*	*310.9*	*1,750.7*
Office of Fire and Aviation	91.1	0	91.1
No state	275.1	22.2	297.3
Total	**1,714.9**	**333.1**	**2,048.1**

Source: Data provided by the Bureau of Land Management, Budget Division, July 22, 2014. Adapted by CRS.

Notes: This table shows appropriations to BLM state offices, which in some cases administer lands (and/or onshore federal minerals) in more than one state. Specifically, the eastern states office administers lands in states east of the Mississippi River; the Montana office administers lands in Montana, North Dakota, and South Dakota; the New Mexico office administers lands in Kansas, New Mexico, Oklahoma, and Texas; the Oregon office administers lands in Oregon and Washington; and the Wyoming office administers lands in Nebraska and Wyoming. The Office of Fire and Aviation is a national-level office. "No state" refers to appropriations for BLM operations that are not applied to a state office, such as appropriations for the BLM headquarters in Washington, DC.

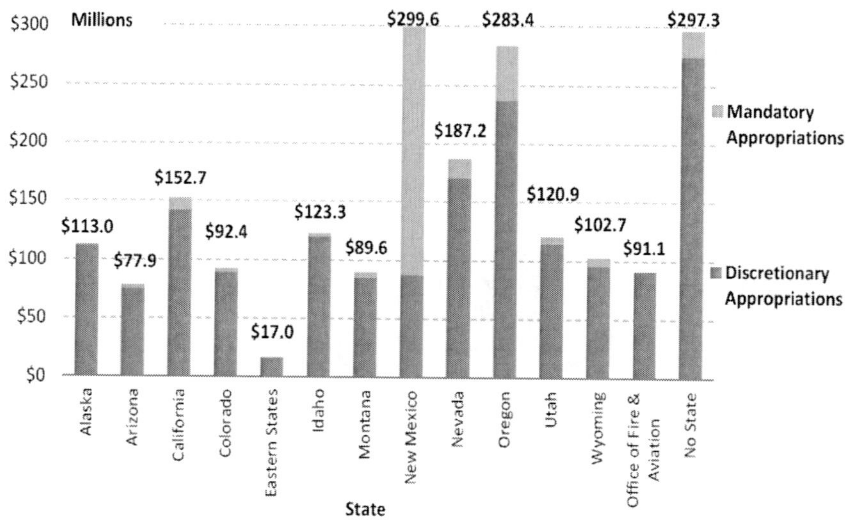

Source: Prepared by CRS with data from the Bureau of Land Management, Budget Division, July 22, 2014. Adapted by CRS.

Notes: See notes to Table 1.

Figure 3. Bureau of Land Management Appropriations by State, FY2013; (in millions of dollars).

Table 2. Bureau of Land Management Discretionary Appropriations by State, FY2013 (in millions of dollars)

	Management of Lands and Resources[a]	Wildland Fire Management	Oregon and California Grant Lands	Working Capital Fund	Service Charges, Deposits, and Forfeitures	Land Acquisition	Total Discretionary Appropriations
Alaska	58.4	48.9	0	0.4	4.2	0	111.9
Arizona	55.9	14.8	0	3.2	0.7	0.9	75.4
California	82.2	45.1	0	6.6	3.2	5.5	142.5
Colorado	58.9	24.3	0	3.2	0.4	2.2	89.0
Eastern states	15.7	0.9	0	0.3	0.1	0	17.0
Idaho	54.4	53.3	0	12.3	0.4	0.2	120.6
Montana	56.4	20.0	0	2.9	0.6	5.3	85.3
New Mexico	66.7	12.3	0	5.7	3.2	0.1	88.0
Nevada	100.6	57.6	0	6.0	5.9	0	170.1
Oregon	62.0	70.1	94.6	9.0	1.7	0.3	237.8
Utah	72.7	32.3	0	4.8	1.2	3.9	114.9
Wyoming	77.7	10.9	0	4.3	3.2	0	96.1
Subtotal	*764.5*	*478.1*	*94.7*	*59.3*	*24.8*	*18.3*	*1,439.8*
Office of Fire and Aviation	2.9	87.5	0.1	0.6	<0.1	0	91.1
No state	256.4	0	11.3	3.0	1.5	2.8	275.1
Total	**1,020.9**	**478.1**	**106.0**	**62.4**	**26.3**	**21.2**	**1,714.9**

Source: Data provided by the Bureau of Land Management, Budget Division, July 22, 2014. Adapted by CRS.

Notes: See notes to Table 1.

[a] Figures in this column reflect spending authority from offsetting collections, including mining claim holding fees and fees for applications for permits to drill for oil and gas.

Table 3. Bureau of Land Management Mandatory Appropriations by State, FY2013 (in millions of dollars)

	Helium Production Fund	Secure Rural Schools	Land and Resources Management Trust Fund	Recreation Enhancement Fee Program	Permit Processing Improvement Fund	Southern Nevada Public Land Management Act	Range Improvements	Other	Total Mandatory Appropriations
Alaska	0	0	0.6	0.3	0	0	0	0.2	1.1
Arizona	0	0	0.8	1.4	0	0	0.3	<0.1	2.5
California	0	0	6.8	3.2	0	0	0.2	0.1	10.2
Colorado	0	0	0.9	0.7	1.5	0	0.4	<0.1	3.5
Eastern states	0	0	<0.1	<0.1	0	0	0	0	<0.1
Idaho	0	0	0.9	0.9	0	0	0.8	0.1	2.6
Montana	0	0	0.4	0.5	1.4	0	2.0	<0.1	4.3
New Mexico	202.2	0	3.4	0.5	4.3	0	1.2	<0.1	211.5
Nevada	0	0	2.4	4.0	0	8.3	1.1	1.3	17.1
Oregon	0	37.8	2.1	2.3	0	0	0.7	2.7	45.7
Utah	0	0	1.5	3.2	0.5	0	0.7	0.1	6.0
Wyoming	0	0	0.9	0.2	4.3	0	1.2	0.1	6.6
Subtotal	*202.2*	*37.8*	*20.6*	*17.1*	*11.9*	*8.3*	*8.5*	*4.5*	*310.9*
Office of Fire and Aviation	0	0	0	0	0	0	0	0	0
No state	0	0.2	1.2	0.4	4.8	2.3	1.0	12.4	22.2
Total	**202.2**	**38.0**	**21.8**	**17.5**	**16.7**	**10.5**	**9.5**	**16.9**	**333.1**

Source: Data provided by the Bureau of Land Management, Budget Division, July 22, 2014. Adapted by CRS.

Notes: See notes to Table 1. In addition, appropriated entitlements, such as some contributed funds (Land and Resources Management Trust Fund) and Range Improvement funds, are reflected in this table. For appropriated entitlements, the level of spending is controlled by authorizing statutes, but the funding is provided in the annual appropriations acts.

Revenue

Revenue collected by BLM in FY2013 totaled $525.0 million.[35] These monies were derived from a variety of activities and resources on BLM lands, donations, and payments to BLM from other entities. **Table 4** and **Figure 4** show the amount of revenue from each source during FY2013, by state.

BLM sales of helium generated the largest source of revenue—$203.7 million (38.8%) of the total. Mining claim fees, primarily from locatable minerals,[36] brought in the second largest amount, with $67.7 million (12.9%). Rents for varied uses of public lands, such as for communication, solar energy, and wind farm sites, generated $44.4 million (8.5%). Wildland fire reimbursements, which represent payments to BLM for fire work undertaken to assist other federal agencies, were $40.7 million (7.8%). BLM collected $30.9 million (5.9%) in fees from applicants for permits to drill (APD) for oil and gas on federal land. The agency also collected $27.7 million (5.3%) in fees to recover costs of certain activities, such as processing applications for rights of way. Timber receipts from Oregon and California Grant Lands and Coos Bay Wagon Road lands together totaled $25.1 million (4.8%). Other sources of revenue were donations ($22.6 million, 4.3%); fees for recreating on BLM lands ($17.9 million, 3.4%); and proceeds from sale of public domain lands and resources on those lands, for example, timber ($15.9 million, 3.0%). Ten other revenue categories generated the balance of the FY2013 revenue—$28.5 million (5.4%). As shown in **Table 4**, BLM state offices collected widely varying amounts of revenue, ranging from $0.6 million for eastern states to $228.8 million for New Mexico. Many variables affect the level of revenue collected by each state office. They include the amount of lands and onshore federal minerals managed by BLM in the respective states. The types of resources on the lands, such as minerals, timber, and forage, and their availability, affect the level of revenues. Similarly, the kinds of land uses, such as recreation and rights of way, and the frequency and extent of these uses influence collections. Further, while most state offices collected revenues from a variety of land uses and activities, some uses and activities are limited to one or a few states. Some of these uses and activities generated relatively large amounts of revenue in FY2013. For instance, the New Mexico state office collected the most revenue because revenue from the sales of helium—$203.7 million in FY2013—is attributed to that office.[37] Excluding helium sales, the revenue for New Mexico would have been $25.1 million.

Table 4. Bureau of Land Management Revenue by State, FY2013 (in millions of dollars)

	Helium Sales	Mining Claim Fees	Rents for Use of Public Lands	Wildland Fire Reimb.[a]	APD Fees[b]	Cost Recovery Fees	O&C Land Grant Revenues[c]	Trust Fund Donations	Recreation Fees	Public Domain Sales	Other	Total Revenues
Alaska	0	1.2	0.4	15.9	0.1	4.5	0	0.6	0.4	0.1	0.2	23.3
Arizona	0	8.1	4.6	0.1	0	0.8	0	0.9	1.5	1.4	0.6	17.9
California	0	4.7	15.6	0.3	1.4	3.5	0	7.5	3.4	2.5	0.3	39.3
Colorado	0	1.8	1.2	1.1	2.5	0.6	0	1.0	0.7	0.6	0.5	9.9
Eastern states	0	<0.1	0	0	0.3	0.2	0	<0.1	<0.1	<0.1	<0.1	0.6
Idaho	0	3.5	1.4	0.3	0	0.4	0	1.0	0.9	0.1	1.5	9.0
Montana	0	3.0	0.2	0.3	4.2	0.8	0	0.5	0.5	1.6	2.0	13.1
New Mexico	203.7	1.9	2.0	0.1	7.4	3.6	<0.1	3.4	0.5	4.2	2.1	228.8
Nevada	0	30.8	5.6	1.1	0.1	6.3	0	2.7	4.2	2.2	14.4	67.4
Oregon	0	1.2	0.6	0.1	0	1.9	25.1	2.4	2.4	1.2	3.8	38.7
Utah	0	3.7	8.8	0.1	7.9	1.6	0	1.7	3.3	0.9	1.0	28.9
Wyoming	0	7.9	4.0	<0.1	7.2	3.5	0	1.0	0.2	1.2	2.0	27.0
Office of Fire and Aviation	0	0	<0.1	21.3	0	<0.1	0	0	0	0	<0.1	21.3
Total	**203.7**	**67.7**	**44.4**	**40.7**	**30.9**	**27.7**	**25.1**	**22.6**	**17.9**	**15.9**	**28.5**	**525.0**

Source: Data provided by the Bureau of Land Management, Budget Division, July 22, 2014. Adapted by CRS.

Notes: See notes to Table 1.

[a] "Reimb." refers to reimbursements.

[b] "APD" refers to applications for permits to drill.

[c] This column reflects Oregon and California (O&C) Land Grant revenues and Coos Bay Wagon Road revenues.

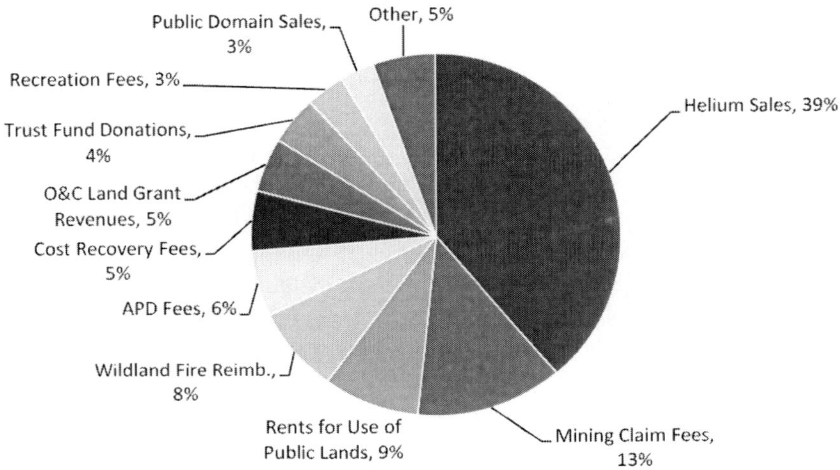

Source: Prepared by CRS with data from the Bureau of Land Management, Budget Division, July 22, 2014.

Notes: The abbreviation "reimb." refers to reimbursements, and the acronym "APD" refers to applications for permits to drill.

Figure 4. Bureau of Land Management Revenue by Type, FY2013.

Similarly, the Oregon state office received virtually all of the $25.1 million in timber revenue from the Oregon and California Grant Lands and Coos Bay Wagon Road lands. This revenue comprised about two-thirds (64.9%) of the revenue for the Oregon state office.

FISH AND WILDLIFE SERVICE

Appropriations

FWS currently estimates that total appropriations for FY2013 were $2,591.6 million.[38] Of this total, $1,538.5 million (59.4%) was discretionary, and $1,053.1 million (40.6%) was mandatory. In contrast to other federal land-managing agencies, only about one-third of FWS appropriations is spent on lands owned by the agency itself.[39] Various grant programs, conservation efforts for migratory birds, and protections of species listed under the Endangered Species Act represent substantial expenditures within a state, but frequently not on FWS lands. Thus, FWS appropriations by state only partly correlate with the amount of agency land in the state. **Table 5** provides the discretionary, mandatory, and total FWS appropriations by state.

Discretionary Appropriations

For FY2013, FWS received $1,538.5 million in discretionary appropriations in 10 accounts, as shown in **Table 6**. The largest discretionary account by far was for Resource Management, which in FY2013 received $1,179.8 million (76.7%) of FWS discretionary appropriations. This account funds an array of FWS programs and activities, including endangered species, National Wildlife Refuge System (NWRS), migratory bird management, and law enforcement. The second largest discretionary appropriation was for Construction ($82.7 million, 5.4%), which funds construction, improvement, and removal of buildings and other facilities. In addition, dam repair, replacement of facilities damaged by disasters, construction of solar arrays, and project design are funded through this account. Supplemental appropriations for Construction, beyond those provided in annual appropriations laws, are sometimes enacted in the wake of natural or man-made disasters.[40] The next-largest accounts in FY2013 were State and Tribal Wildlife Grants ($58.1 million, 3.8%); Wildland Fire Management ($53.0 million, 3.4%); and Land Acquisition ($51.8 million, 3.4%). Other accounts shown in **Table 6** include the Cooperative Endangered Species Conservation Fund ($45.2 million, 2.9%), and the North American Wetlands Conservation Account ($34.1 million, 2.2%).[41]

The three smallest accounts shown in the table merit further explanation. The National Wildlife Refuge Fund (NWRF), though largely dependent on discretionary appropriations, is supported to a limited extent by mandatory appropriations based on national receipt collection.[42] **Table 6** reflects the total appropriation for the NWRF program. In FY2012, the gross receipts were $7.2 million, and this amount was made available without further appropriation in FY2013. The discretionary appropriation was $14.0 million, making a total of $21.2 million (1.4% of discretionary spending) for the NWRF program in FY2013.[43] A portion of the receipts ($3.2 million) was allocated to the expenses involved in managing the revenue-generating activities. The remaining net receipts ($4.0 million) were added to the discretionary appropriation, making $19.0 million (1.2% of discretionary spending) to be allocated to local governments pro rata, based on a statutory formula.

Appropriations for the other two small accounts, the Multinational Species Conservation Fund ($9.0 million, 0.6% of discretionary spending) and the Neotropical Migratory Bird Conservation Fund ($3.6 million, 0.2%), are both spent primarily in other nations.[44] They are included in the total for Virginia, where FWS national headquarters is located and through which such appropriations are allocated.

Mandatory Appropriations

A variety of laws provide for mandatory appropriations for FWS. Of the $1,053.1 million provided under these laws in FY2013, the largest amounts were from a pair of funds: the Wildlife Restoration Fund ($534.2 million, 50.7% of all FWS mandatory spending) and the Sportfish Restoration Fund ($439.1 million, 41.7%).[45] See **Table 7**. Together, they were 92.4% of all FWS mandatory appropriations in FY2013. These two programs provide for formula-based grants to states and territories for the conservation of game and sportfish, respectively. The two programs are funded by excise taxes on guns, revolvers, ammunition, bows, and arrows in the case of the Wildlife Restoration Fund and on rods, reels, motorboat fuel, and other fishing equipment for the Sportfish Restoration Fund. A much smaller mandatory appropriation is the Migratory Bird Conservation Account (MBCA, $65.0 million, 6.2%), funded largely by the sale of duck stamps and by import duties on arms and ammunition.[46] The MBCA funds the acquisition of lands and interests in lands to benefit habitat for migratory waterfowl and upland game birds.

The collections in these three funds during one year are available, without further appropriation, to FWS in the following year.[47] FWS spends the funds without regard to the state in which they were collected.

In FY2013, there were three additional mandatory appropriations. One was the Recreation Fee Enhancement Program, which allows FWS sites to collect entrance and other fees and use them to enhance visitor experiences. The program affected 164 sites in FY2013, with total collections of $5.0 million (0.5% of mandatory appropriations). The second appropriation, Contributed Funds, derives from voluntary contributions from state governments and other entities to support specified conservation activities. Amounts may vary from year to year, and totaled $5.0 million (0.5% of mandatory appropriations) in FY2013. Third, Miscellaneous Permanent Appropriations includes several appropriations that totaled $4.9 million (0.5%) in FY2013. Most of the funding was derived from rental fees for FWS staff quarters, generally in isolated locations, and was used for operation and maintenance of those quarters. Other programs funded by Miscellaneous Permanent Appropriations were management activities on Army Corps of Engineers lands managed by FWS, certain lands in Nevada, and other areas.

Discussion

FWS owns or manages land in all 50 states, four territories, and in minor outlying islands that are not part of any territory. In addition, the agency spends funds in the District of Columbia and the Commonwealth of the Northern Mariana Islands even though there are no FWS lands in those jurisdictions. Among the states, the FY2013 appropriation for Virginia was the largest ($264.6 million), given the presence of the agency's headquarters. California, with a number of refuges, major state grants, and a variety of conflicts concerning endangered species and water management, received the second-largest appropriation ($169.7 million). Alaska, having by far the largest acreage in the NWRS, was next ($149.5 million). Other states with over $100 million in FY2013 appropriations were Georgia ($112.0 million), Minnesota ($105.4 million), and Oregon ($100.4 million). By contrast, jurisdictions with FY2013 appropriations under $5 million were Midway Islands ($4.1 million), Guam ($3.6 million), Commonwealth of the Northern Mariana Islands ($2.5 million), American Samoa ($2.2 million), and Virgin Islands ($2.2 million).

The level of appropriations allocated by FWS to various states is influenced by a number of factors. One is the amount of land managed by FWS, which varies widely among states.[48] For instance, while some states have relatively large amounts of FWS land, the District of Columbia has none and Connecticut, Rhode Island, and the Virgin Islands have among the least. Different land resources, conditions, uses, and impacts can affect the cost of land management, as can demographics. Another variable is the cost of travel, with Alaska, Hawaii, and outlying islands, among others, having high operating costs due in part to the expense of staff travel to these locations.

Other factors influencing spending are the number of species listed under the Endangered Species Act, the presence of wetlands, entry ports for regulated wildlife, and other programs. Still other differences can arise from the two major grant programs with mandatory appropriations: the Wildlife Restoration Program and the Sportfish Restoration Program. The allocation of funds for both depends on a statutory formula based on the area of the state and the number of licensed hunters or fishers, respectively. Thus, large states with many hunters and fishers will receive larger amounts of funding, while small states with few hunters and few fishers will receive relatively little.

Table 5. Fish and Wildlife Service Appropriations by State, FY2013 (in millions of dollars)

	Discretionary Appropriations	Mandatory Appropriations	Total Appropriations
Alabama	7.3	19.4	26.7
Alaska	108.2	41.3	149.5
Arizona	17.5	20.2	37.7
Arkansas	11.6	15.9	27.5
California	123.2	46.5	169.7
Colorado	73.1	26.5	99.7
Connecticut	3.6	7.4	11.1
Delaware	22.5	7.7	30.2
District of Columbia	17.1	1.2	18.3
Florida	48.1	22.0	70.1
Georgia	79.7	32.4	112.0
Hawaii	29.9	7.7	37.5
Idaho	15.3	16.0	31.3
Illinois	13.4	18.6	32.1
Indiana	5.4	13.8	19.2
Iowa	8.7	14.5	23.3
Kansas	6.9	14.7	21.6
Kentucky	4.4	14.4	18.8
Louisiana	18.7	20.6	39.3
Maine	10.6	9.5	20.1
Maryland	13.0	9.7	22.6
Massachusetts	58.1	22.3	80.4
Michigan	16.1	29.0	45.1
Minnesota	63.4	42.0	105.4
Mississippi	13.8	11.5	25.3
Missouri	8.5	23.2	31.8
Montana	26.8	23.5	50.2
Nebraska	9.0	12.8	21.8
Nevada	12.7	14.3	26.9
New Hampshire	4.1	7.6	11.7
New Jersey	30.9	8.9	39.8
New Mexico	59.0	19.1	78.0
New York	17.8	26.1	43.8
North Carolina	20.9	24.7	45.6
North Dakota	24.4	28.5	52.9
Ohio	4.3	18.5	22.7
Oklahoma	12.6	18.6	31.3
Oregon	70.2	30.2	100.4

Table 5. (Continued)

	Discretionary Appropriations	Mandatory Appropriations	Total Appropriations
Pennsylvania	7.2	27.1	34.2
Rhode Island	3.9	6.7	10.6
South Carolina	11.5	16.1	27.6
South Dakota	14.3	32.2	46.5
Tennessee	12.7	19.4	32.1
Texas	45.7	47.1	92.8
Utah	9.9	17.0	26.9
Vermont	4.3	6.8	11.1
Virginiaa	215.5	49.1	264.6
Washington	48.7	18.1	66.8
West Virginia	28.0	9.1	37.1
Wisconsin	18.9	28.2	47.0
Wyoming	8.0	15.1	23.1
American Samoa	0.1	2.0	2.2
Guam	1.6	2.0	3.6
Northern Mariana Islands	0.4	2.0	2.5
Puerto Rico	7.4	5.8	13.2
Virgin Islands	0.1	2.0	2.2
Midway Islandsb	3.8	0.3	4.1
Unallocated geographyc	5.5	6.2	11.7
Total	1,538.5	1,053.1	2,591.6

Source: Data provided by Chris Nolin, Budget Division, Fish and Wildlife Service, July 18, 2014. Adapted by CRS.

Notes:

[a] Figures for Virginia reflect the presence of FWS national headquarters.

[b] Midway Islands are shown separately because they are not considered part of any state or territory.

[c] Unallocated geography reflects certain offshore expenditures in Minor Outlying Islands, primarily in the Pacific Ocean.

Table 6. Fish and Wildlife Service Discretionary Appropriations by State, FY2013 (in millions of dollars)

	Resource Mgmt.	Construction	State and Tribal Wildlife Grants	Wildland Fire Mgmt.	Land Acquisition	Cooperative Endangered Species Conserv. Fund	North Amer. Wetlands Conserv. Account	Natl. Wildlife Refuge Fund	Multinatl. Species Conserv. Fund	Neotropical Migratory Bird Conserv. Fund	State Totals
Alabama	6.2	0	0.7	<0.1	0	0.4	0	<0.1	0	0	7.3
Alaska	100.1	0.7	2.8	2.3	2.1	0.1	0	0.1	0	0	108.2
Arizona	14.5	0	1.2	1.4	0	0.4	0	0	0	0	17.5
Arkansas	9.1	0	0.5	0.2	0	1.3	0.3	0.1	0	0	11.6
California	93.0	<0.1	3.1	4.2	3.4	15.3	3.0	1.1	0	0	123.2
Colorado	61.8	1.0	1.6	1.5	1.0	0.6	1.9	3.8	0	0	73.1
Connecticut	0.6	1.0	0.5	0	1.6	0	0	0	0	0	3.6
Delaware	2.3	19.7	0.5	0	0	0	0	0	0	0	22.5
District of Columbia	16.9	0	0.2	0	0	0	0	0	0	0	17.1
Florida	35.5	<0.1	2.1	3.5	4.0	2.8	0	0.1	0	0	48.1
Georgia	48.7	0.9	2.2	3.5	13.4	1.6	0	9.3	0	0	79.7
Hawaii	26.3	0	0.5	0	0	3.1	0	0	0	0	29.9
Idaho	11.8	0	0.6	2.7	0	0.2	0	<0.1	0	0	15.3
Illinois	10.9	0.3	1.5	0.6	0	0	0	0.1	0	0	13.4
Indiana	4.0	0	0.8	0.3	0	0.3	0	0	0	0	5.4
Iowa	5.8	0	0.6	0.4	1.0	0	1.0	0	0	0	8.7
Kansas	5.4	0	0.7	0.8	0	<0.1	0	<0.1	0	0	6.9
Kentucky	2.6	0	0.6	<0.1	1.0	0.2	0	0	0	0	4.4
Louisiana	16.8	0	0.7	0.7	0	0.1	0.3	0.1	0	0	18.7
Maine	9.3	0.6	0.5	0.2	0	0	0	0	0	0	10.6
Maryland	11.1	0.7	0.6	0.5	0	0	0	<0.1	0	0	13.0

Table 6. (Continued)

	Resource Mgmt.	Construction	State and Tribal Wildlife Grants	Wildland Fire Mgmt.	Land Acquisition	Cooperative Endangered Species Conserv. Fund	North Amer. Wetlands Conserv. Account	Natl. Wildlife Refuge Fund	Multinatl. Species Conserv. Fund	Neotropical Migratory Bird Conserv. Fund	State Totals
Massachusetts	40.9	5.8	2.7	1.3	4.8	0.1	0	2.5	0	0	58.1
Michigan	10.0	4.4	1.3	0.2	0	0.3	0	0	0	0	16.1
Minnesota	48.6	2.1	3.5	3.5	2.7	0.1	1.0	1.9	0	0	63.4
Mississippi	10.4	0	0.5	1.3	0	0.1	1.3	<0.1	0	0	13.8
Missouri	7.2	0	0.9	0.1	0	0.3	0	0	0	0	8.5
Montana	23.5	0	0.8	0.8	1.5	0.1	0	0.1	0	0	26.8
Nebraska	6.8	0	0.6	0.4	0	0.2	1.0	<0.1	0	0	9.0
Nevada	11.1	0	0.8	0.3	0	0.5	0	0	0	0	12.7
New Hampshire	3.7	<0.1	0.5	0	0	0	0	<0.1	0	0	4.1
New Jersey	7.4	22.0	0.9	0.2	0	0.4	0	0	0	0	30.9
New Mexico	50.2	0.7	1.4	2.5	3.2	0.4	0	0.6	0	0	59.0
New York	10.8	4.7	2.2	<0.1	0	0	0	0	0	0	17.8
North Carolina	12.1	5.8	1.2	1.5	0	0.3	0	0	0	0	20.9
North Dakota	17.1	0	0.5	1.2	3.2	0.1	2.0	0.4	0	0	24.4
Ohio	2.9	0	1.3	<0.1	0	0	0	0	0	0	4.3
Oklahoma	10.7	0	0.7	1.0	0	0.1	0	0.1	0	0	12.6
Oregon	58.5	1.1	2.0	2.6	3.2	1.4	1.0	0.3	0	0	70.2
Pennsylvania	5.4	<0.1	1.5	<0.1	0	0.2	0	0	0	0	7.2
Rhode Island	1.8	1.4	0.5	0.2	0	0	0	0	0	0	3.9
South Carolina	9.4	0	0.6	1.4	0	0.1	0	<0.1	0	0	11.5
South Dakota	10.9	0	0.5	0.8	0.1	<0.1	2.0	<0.1	0	0	14.3
Tennessee	10.8	0	0.8	<0.1	0	1.0	0	<0.1	0	0	12.7
Texas	36.8	0	1.0	4.6	1.0	2.2	0	0.2	0	0	45.7

	Resource Mgmt.	Construction	State and Tribal Wildlife Grants	Wildland Fire Mgmt.	Land Acquisition	Cooperative Endangered Species Conserv. Fund	North Amer. Wetlands Conserv. Account	Natl. Wildlife Refuge Fund	Multinatl. Species Conserv. Fund	Neotropical Migratory Bird Conserv. Fund	State Totals
Utah	7.3	0	0.7	0.4	0	1.5	0	<0.1	0	0	9.9
Vermont	2.9	0.9	0.5	0	0	0	0	0	0	0	4.3
Virginia[a]	170.1	7.2	1.1	2.2	3.5	1.4	17.2	0.2	9.0	3.6	215.5
Washington	38.8	0.2	1.0	2.0	1.0	5.6	0	0.1	0	0	48.7
West Virginia	26.0	1.5	0.5	<0.1	0	0	0	0	0	0	28.0
Wisconsin	15.4	0	0.8	0.8	0	0.7	1.2	0	0	0	18.9
Wyoming	6.5	0	0.5	<0.1	0	0.1	0.8	0	0	0	8.0
American Samoa	0	0	0.1	0	0	0	0	0	0	0	0.1
Guam	1.1	0	0.1	0	0	0.3	0	0	0	0	1.6
Northern Mariana Islands	0	0	0.1	0	0	0.3	0	0	0	0	0.4
Puerto Rico	6.7	0	0.2	0.2	0	0.3	0	0	0	0	7.4
Virgin Islands	<0.1	0	0.1	0	0	0	0	0	0	0	0.1
Midway Islands[b]	3.8	0	0	0	0	0	0	0	0	0	3.8
Unallocated geography[c]	1.6	0	3.2	0.3	0	0.4	0	0	0	0	5.5
Total	1,179.8	82.7	58.1	53.0	51.8	45.2	34.1[d]	21.2[e]	9.0	3.6	1,538.5

Source: Data provided by the Fish and Wildlife Service, Budget Division, July 18, 2014. Adapted by CRS.

Notes:

[a] Figures for Virginia reflect the presence of FWS headquarters.

[b] Midway Islands are not considered part of any state or territory.

[c] Unallocated geography reflects certain offshore expenditures in minor outlying islands, primarily in the Pacific Ocean.

[d] This total includes $475,000 in fines under the Migratory Bird Treaty Act. Although this funding is mandatory, it is included here because the amount is very small.

[e] This total includes $7.2 million in gross receipts collected on NWRS lands in FY2012 and made available for expenditure in FY2013. Although this funding is mandatory, it is reflected here because it is relatively small. However, it is discussed in the section on “Revenue.”

Table 7. Fish and Wildlife Service Mandatory Appropriations by State, FY2013 (in millions of dollars)

	Wildlife Restoration	Sportfish Restoration	Migratory Bird Conservation Account	Contributed Funds	Recreation Fee Enhancement Program	Miscellaneous Permanent Appropriations	State Totals
Alabama	12.7	6.6	0	0	<0.1	0.1	19.4
Alaska	21.9	18.0	0	0.3	0.2	0.9	41.3
Arizona	13.0	7.0	0	0	<0.1	0.2	20.2
Arkansas	9.6	6.1	0	0	0.1	<0.1	15.9
California	19.3	22.1	4.4	0.1	0.1	0.5	46.5
Colorado	13.8	9.4	3.1	0.1	<0.1	0.1	26.5
Connecticut	3.9	3.5	0	0	<0.1	0	7.4
Delaware	3.1	4.5	0	0	<0.1	0	7.7
District of Columbia	0	1.2	0	0	0	0	1.2
Florida	9.3	11.8	0	0.1	0.7	0.1	22.0
Georgia	12.6	18.5	0.9	0.1	0.1	0.2	32.4
Hawaii	3.1	3.5	0	0.2	0.7	0.1	7.7
Idaho	9.7	6.2	0	<0.1	<0.1	0.1	16.0
Illinois	11.0	7.1	0	<0.1	0.4	0.1	18.6
Indiana	9.1	4.7	0	0	<0.1	<0.1	13.8
Iowa	8.7	4.6	1.1	0	<0.1	<0.1	14.5
Kansas	9.3	5.0	0	0	<0.1	0.3	14.7
Kentucky	9.1	5.3	0	0	<0.1	<0.1	14.4
Louisiana	9.9	8.4	2.1	<0.1	0.2	<0.1	20.6
Maine	5.7	3.7	0	0.1	<0.1	<0.1	9.5

	Wildlife Restoration	Sportfish Restoration	Migratory Bird Conservation Account	Contributed Funds	Recreation Fee Enhancement Program	Miscellaneous Permanent Appropriations	State Totals
Maryland	5.1	3.6	0.8	<0.1	<0.1	0.1	9.7
Massachusetts	6.1	14.8	1.0	0.1	0.2	0.1	22.3
Michigan	17.0	11.9	0	0.1	<0.1	<0.1	29.0
Minnesota	17.3	18.4	5.3	0.9	0	<0.1	42.0
Mississippi	7.0	4.2	<0.1	0.1	0.1	<0.1	11.5
Missouri	14.9	8.2	0	0.1	<0.1	<0.1	23.2
Montana	13.6	8.4	1.3	<0.1	<0.1	0.1	23.5
Nebraska	8.4	4.4	0	<0.1	0	<0.1	12.8
Nevada	9.0	5.2	0	0	0	0.1	14.3
New Hampshire	3.1	4.5	0	0	0	<0.1	7.6
New Jersey	5.2	3.5	0	0.1	<0.1	0.1	8.9
New Mexico	10.7	7.6	0.6	0	0.1	0.1	19.1
New York	14.0	9.5	2.3	0.2	<0.1	0.1	26.1
North Carolina	13.5	11.1	0	0.1	<0.1	<0.1	24.7
North Dakota	8.9	3.9	15.2	0.3	<0.1	0.1	28.5
Ohio	11.2	7.2	0	0.1	<0.1	<0.1	18.5
Oklahoma	11.4	7.2	0	0	<0.1	0.1	18.6
Oregon	12.1	17.4	0.4	0.1	0	0.2	30.2
Pennsylvania	18.9	8.2	0	0	<0.1	0	27.1
Rhode Island	3.1	3.5	0	0	<0.1	0	6.7
South Carolina	6.6	7.9	1.5	<0.1	0.1	<0.1	16.1

Table 7. (Continued)

	Wildlife Restoration	Sportfish Restoration	Migratory Bird Conservation Account	Contributed Funds	Recreation Fee Enhancement Program	Miscellaneous Permanent Appropriations	State Totals
South Dakota	9.3	4.3	18.5	0	0	<0.1	32.2
Tennessee	12.9	6.4	0	<0.1	<0.1	0	19.4
Texas	23.6	20.5	2.6	0.1	0.2	0.1	47.1
Utah	9.3	6.4	1.2	<0.1	0	<0.1	17.0
Vermont	3.1	3.5	0	0.2	0	<0.1	6.8
Virginiaa	17.6	27.3	2.1	1.0	0.9	0.2	49.1
Washington	10.0	7.2	0.5	<0.1	0.2	0.2	18.1
West Virginia	5.6	3.5	0	<0.1	<0.1	<0.1	9.1
Wisconsin	16.0	12.1	0	0.1	<0.1	<0.1	28.2
Wyoming	9.2	5.4	0	0.3	0.1	0.1	15.1
American	0.9	1.2	0	0	0	0	2.0
Samoa							
Guam	0.9	1.2	0	0	0	0	2.0
Northern	0.9	1.2	0	0	0	0	2.0
Mariana							
Islands							
Puerto Rico	2.2	3.5	0	0	0	0	5.8
Virgin Islands	0.9	1.2	0	0	<0.1	0	2.0
Midway	0	0	0	0	0	0.3	0.3
Islandsb							

	Wildlife Restoration	Sportfish Restoration	Migratory Bird Conservation Account	Contributed Funds	Recreation Fee Enhancement Program	Miscellaneous Permanent Appropriations	State Totals
Unallocated	0	6.2	0	0	0	0	6.2
Geographyc							
Total	**534.2**	**439.1**	**65.0**	**5.0**	**5.0d**	**4.9**	**1,053.1**

Source: Data provided by the Fish and Wildlife Service, Budget Division, July 18, 2014. Adapted by CRS. Notes:

[a] Figures for Virginia reflect the presence of FWS national headquarters.

[b] Midway Islands are not considered part of any state or territory.

[c] Unallocated geography reflects certain offshore expenditures in minor outlying islands, primarily in the Pacific Ocean.

[d] As noted in the "Introduction" section of this report, figures throughout the report may not add to totals shown due to rounding. This is the case with the figures in this column, due in part to the large number of figures reflected as <0.1.

Revenue

Revenues associated with FWS can be divided into two categories. First are those that are collected by the Treasury Department, then transferred and made available without further appropriation to FWS for expenditure in the following year. In this category there are three programs: the large Wildlife Restoration and Sportfish Restoration programs, funded by excise taxes on hunting and fishing equipment, respectively, and the somewhat smaller Migratory Bird Conservation Account, funded by the sale of duck stamps and by import duties on arms and ammunition. In all three cases, revenues are devoted to program activities, with a small set-aside for program administration. In general, collection of these revenues cannot be attributed by FWS to a particular state. Moreover, their expenditure is unrelated to the state where they were collected. (See the section "Mandatory Appropriations" above regarding all three programs.)

In the second category are revenues collected by FWS itself. The agency collects relatively little revenue directly as compared with other land management agencies covered in this report. Nationally, for FY2013, FWS collected $18.9 million in revenues.[49] Under law, activities in the NWRS must be compatible with the purposes for which the refuge was designated.[50] As a result, few commercial activities are permitted on lands in the NWRS unless the activities benefit wildlife conservation. For a number of years, it has been the policy of FWS gradually to eliminate preexisting incompatible uses from refuges, except in cases of valid existing rights over which the agency has no control.[51] With few permitted commercial activities, very little revenue is usually collected in the NWRS. Because the revenue generated from these four sources is relatively small, no state breakdowns are provided in this section.

The FY2013 revenue collected by FWS derives from four sources, as shown in **Figure 5**. They are:

- Recreation fees ($5.0 million) are used largely or entirely at the refuges where they are collected.[52] On refuges where collections are substantial, the effects on those refuges may also be substantial.
- Funds contributed for special projects at specific sites ($5.0 million) may be used in the year of the donation or in subsequent years, depending on the nature of the project, planning time, permits, and similar variables.

- Miscellaneous permanent receipts ($4.9 million) are authorized by multiple statutes with different rules about availability of funds in the year of deposit or in subsequent years.[53]
- Funds were collected at refuges for certain commercial activities in FY2012, and the net amount was paid into the National Wildlife Refuge Fund in FY2013 ($4.0 million in net revenues). The receipts are derived from the sale of products, such as timber or gravel; rights of way; grazing permits; and leases for accommodations (such as those built for oil and gas exploration or development). Any given refuge may have all, few, or none of these activities.

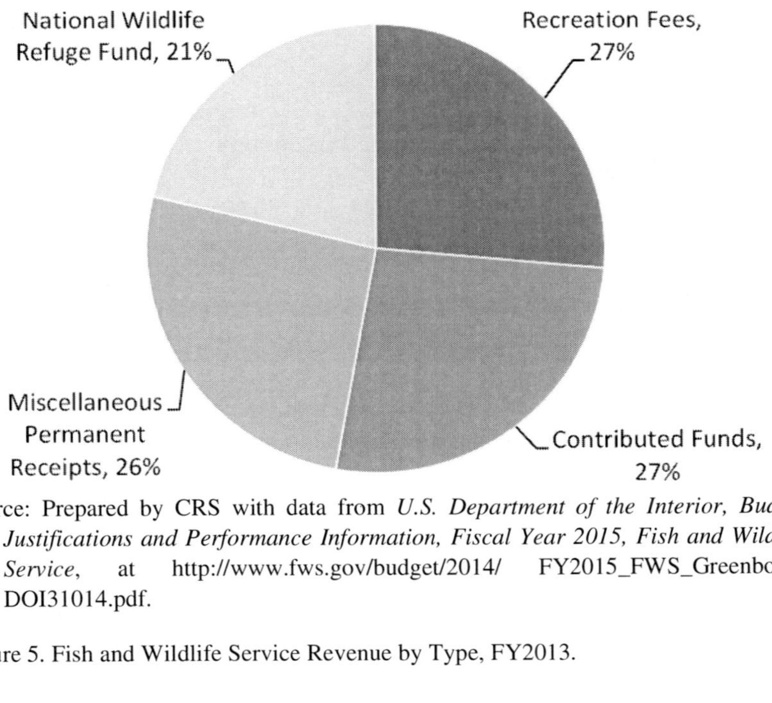

Source: Prepared by CRS with data from *U.S. Department of the Interior, Budget Justifications and Performance Information, Fiscal Year 2015, Fish and Wildlife Service*, at http://www.fws.gov/budget/2014/ FY2015_FWS_Greenbook-DOI31014.pdf.

Figure 5. Fish and Wildlife Service Revenue by Type, FY2013.

NATIONAL PARK SERVICE

Appropriations

The National Park Service (NPS) estimates that its discretionary appropriations for FY2013 were $2,885.2 million,[54] and its mandatory appropriations were $420.6 million,[55] for a total FY2013 appropriation of $3,305.8 million. Discretionary appropriations constituted 87.3% of the total, and mandatory appropriations constituted 12.7%. The FY2013 appropriations were distributed across all 50 states, the District of Columbia, and eight U.S. territories or associated states.

NPS appropriations were used both to manage agency-owned lands and to assist managers of nonfederal lands with preservation and recreation activities. Although the NPS administers many programs for nonfederal assistance, the great majority of agency appropriations go to federal units of the National Park System. One discretionary account used for agency lands—the Operation of the National Park System account—alone received over three-fifths of all NPS appropriations in FY2013.

Discretionary Appropriations

Table 8 shows the Park Service's FY2013 discretionary appropriations, by account, for each state or other area. The discretionary total of $2,885.2 million covered five accounts specific to the NPS, as well as funds allocated from a DOI department-wide account for Wildland Fire Management.[56] Nearly three-quarters of the appropriations ($2,097.3 million, or 71.9%)[57] went to the Operation of the National Park System (ONPS) account, which supports the day-to-day operations of the parks. Activities covered by this account include visitor services, natural and cultural resource stewardship, facility operations and maintenance, and park protection, among others. The majority of funds are provided directly to managers of individual park units.

The second-largest amount was $453.9 million (15.6%) for Construction. This account funds new construction projects as well as repairs and improvements to existing facilities. In FY2013, the appropriation included supplemental funding of $329.8 million[58] in P.L. 113-2 for response to and recovery from Superstorm Sandy, which severely damaged park units on the East Coast. Another $110.2 million (3.8%) was allocated to the NPS from DOI's department-wide account for Wildland Fire Management.

A total of $100.5 million (3.4%) was appropriated for the Historic Preservation Fund (HPF) account, which assists states and localities with the conservation of cultural and historical sites and assets. This total included supplemental funding of $47.5 million[59] in P.L. 113-2 for Superstorm Sandy disaster relief. Funding is distributed to states and territories on a formula basis. State and tribal historic preservation offices administer the HPF grants, which normally require a 60% federal/40% state match.

The Land Acquisition and State Assistance account, containing NPS's share of appropriations from the Land and Water Conservation Fund (LWCF), received $96.6 million (3.3%).[60] These appropriations fund both NPS land acquisition and assistance to states for outdoor recreation purposes. The National Recreation and Preservation account, which provides assistance to state, local, tribal, and private land managers, received $56.7 million (1.9%). The largest single program contained in this account is for NPS assistance to national heritage areas.[61]

Mandatory Appropriations

The NPS does not track mandatory appropriations by state, and thus no table of NPS mandatory appropriations is provided in this report. In FY2013, the agency received an overall total of $420.6 million from 16 mandatory appropriations, primarily composed of agency receipts.[62] Most of the receipts were retained for use in the states in which they were collected; thus, the breakdown of NPS revenue collections by state in **Table 9** may give some general sense of the geographic distribution of the agency's mandatory appropriations. However, there are significant differences between the revenues collected and the mandatory appropriations for each state. First, although park units in each state retain most of the revenues they collect, they do not retain them all; different amounts are deposited in a central fund depending on the type of revenue and other circumstances (see below). Second, in FY2013 the amount of collected revenues actually available to the states was reduced by budget sequestration, which is not reflected in the revenue table. Third, in addition to the revenue programs shown in **Table 9**, the NPS has some additional mandatory appropriations that do not come from revenues collected by the agency and thus are not shown in the table.[63] Given these differences, it is not possible to closely estimate each state's mandatory appropriation from the revenue amounts.

The largest source of NPS mandatory appropriations in FY2013 was the Recreation Fee Program, authorized under the Federal Lands Recreation Enhancement Act (FLREA).[64] The act allows the NPS to charge fees for entrance to park units and for certain recreational activities. Between 60% and 100% of the fees collected under the act are retained for use at the collecting park, while the remainder are placed in a central account and may be used elsewhere in the system (for example, at parks with no fee collections).[65] In FY2013, NPS mandatory appropriations from recreation fees totaled $177.7 million, or 42.2% of all mandatory appropriations.[66] Almost all the states collected recreation fees and retained funding from the program.

The next-largest source of NPS mandatory appropriations was the Concession Franchise Fee program, consisting of fees paid to the agency by concessioners.[67] Mandatory appropriations from this program totaled $64.5 million in FY2013 (15.3%), and involved most of the states.

Other sources of mandatory appropriations included the Contribution for Annuity Benefits for U.S. Park Police, with $45.1 million (10.7%), consisting of funds warranted to the NPS from a permanent, indefinite appropriation at the Treasury Department for certain police retirement benefits; Donations, with $39.3 million (9.3%), consisting of direct cash donations to the Park Service; Operation and Maintenance of Quarters, $21.3 million (5.1%), comprising rents and charges for employee use of government housing and amenities; the Transportation Systems Fund, with $16.2 million (3.9%), covering fees for the use of public transportation services within the National Park System; Concessions Improvement Accounts of $14.2 million (3.4%), consisting of monies for facility improvements paid by some concessioners under a program that is being phased out; and the Park Buildings Lease and Maintenance Fund with $6.3 million (1.5%), composed of rents from leases on NPS buildings and other property under various provisions of law, among others.

Discussion

Units of the National Park System exist in all 50 states,[68] the District of Columbia, and several territories.[69] The agency also provides assistance to nonfederal land managers in all the states and other areas. Accordingly, funds from several NPS accounts—such as the ONPS account for park operations, the Historic Preservation Fund for state and local preservation activities, and the Land and Water Conservation Fund, which includes state assistance grants—have very broad geographic distribution.[70]

The appropriated amounts vary considerably by state and from year to year within a given state. The distribution of NPS funding across states is related to the amount of land administered by NPS in each state but also influenced by many other factors. Although Alaska contains far and away the greatest portion of NPS lands—nearly two-thirds of the acreage of the entire system— several states (California, Colorado, New York, and Pennsylvania) and the District of Columbia received higher appropriations than Alaska in FY2013.

Table 8. National Park Service Discretionary Appropriations by State, FY2013 (in millions of dollars)

	Operation of the NPS	Construction	Wildland Fire Management	Historic Preservation Fund	Land Acquisition and State Assistance	National Recreation and Preservation	Total Discretionary
Alabama	5.9	0	0.9	0.8	0.6	0.2	8.3
Alaska	61.6	14.9	5.0	1.0	0.4	1.0	83.8
Arizona	59.2	0.9	6.5	0.8	5.8	0	73.2
Arkansas	14.0	0	0.8	0.7	0.5	0	16.0
California	170.6	9.0	51.7	1.4	5.4	2.8	240.9
Colorado	55.1	28.5	14.9	0.8	0.7	6.9	107.0
Connecticut	1.3	0	0	8.7	0.6	0.7	11.3
Delaware	0[a]	0	0	0.5	0.4	0	0.9
Dist. of Columbia	793.1	18.2	0.3	1.0	27.8	16.8	857.2
Florida	50.4	12.8	4.3	1.0	1.8	0.2	70.4
Georgia	31.1	1.8	1.8	0.9	1.0	4.1	40.6
Hawaii	24.0	0.1	0.6	0.6	0.4	0	25.7
Idaho	7.9	0	3.0	0.7	0.4	0	11.9
Illinois	3.2	0	0	1.1	1.4	0.7	6.4
Indiana	10.3	0	1.1	0.9	0.8	0	13.1
Iowa	2.4	0	0	0.8	0.5	0	3.7
Kansas	5.2	0	0	0.8	0.5	0.3	6.8
Kentucky	10.4	0	0.4	0.8	0.6	0	12.2
Louisiana	7.4	0	0	0.8	0.7	2.2	11.0
Maine	9.1	0	0.4	0.7	0.4	0	10.6
Maryland	34.7	7.4	<0.1	0.8	0.8	0.2	43.8
Massachusetts	41.5	5.7	0.4	0.9	0.9	0.5	49.9
Michigan	13.1	0	0	1.0	1.1	0.4	15.7
Minnesota	9.0	0	0.4	0.9	0.7	0	11.0
Mississippi	16.3	0	0	0.7	0.5	0.3	17.8

Table 8. (Continued)

	Operation of the NPS	Construction	Wildland Fire Management	Historic Preservation Fund	Land Acquisition and State Assistance	National Recreation and Preservation	Total Discretionary
Missouri	22.3	<0.1	0.7	0.9	0.7	0	24.8
Montana	21.2	0.4	0.7	0.7	1.6	0	24.7
Nebraska	16.6	1.9	1.5	0.7	0.4	3.8	24.9
Nevada	15.3	0	<0.1	0.7	0.5	0.2	16.7
New Hampshire	1.4	0	0	0.6	0.4	0	2.3
New Jersey	14.9	36.9	0.5	14.0	1.1	0.3	67.7
New Mexico	24.3	0.5	3.8	0.7	0.5	0.2	30.0
New York	96.1	275.1	0	14.9	1.9	0.6	388.6
North Carolina	30.0	7.0	1.1	0.9	0.9	0.6	40.5
North Dakota	4.2	0	0.3	0.7	0.4	0	5.6
Ohio	16.7	0.3	0	1.0	1.2	0	19.2
Oklahoma	5.0	0	0.1	0.8	0.6	0	6.5
Oregon	9.9	0	0.4	0.8	0.6	0	11.8
Pennsylvania	82.6	3.6	0.7	1.1	1.3	10.7	99.9
Rhode Island	0.7	0	0	3.8	0.4	0.3	5.2
South Carolina	6.7	0.2	0.1	0.7	0.6	0	8.4
South Dakota	12.3	3.0	1.1	0.7	0.4	0	17.4
Tennessee	23.8	0.1	<0.1	0.8	0.7	0	25.5
Texas	35.7	<0.1	3.0	1.2	2.2	0	42.1
Utah	30.9	0.1	1.3	0.7	0.5	0.3	33.8
Vermont	1.9	0	0	0.6	0.3	0	2.8
Virginia	61.5	4.0	0.9	0.8	0.9	0	68.1
Washington	40.2	2.2	1.6	0.9	1.8	0	46.7
West Virginia	16.6	9.8	0.2	0.7	0.4	0	27.6
Wisconsin	7.1	0	0	0.9	0.7	0	8.7

	Operation of the NPS	Construction	Wildland Fire Management	Historic Preservation Fund	Land Acquisition and State Assistance	National Recreation and Preservation	Total Discretionary
Wyoming	46.9	9.2	1.0	0.7	8.4	0	66.2
American Samoa	1.8	0	0	0.4	<0.1	0	2.3
FS of Micronesia	0	0	0	0.4	0	0	0.4
Guam	1.5	0	0	0.4	<0.1	0	1.9
Marshall Islands	0	0	0	0.2	0	0	0.2
N. Mariana Islands	1.5	0	0	0.4	<0.1	0	1.9
Palau	0	0	0	0.2	0	0	0.2
Puerto Rico	3.3	0.2	0	0.6	0.6	0	4.6
Virgin Islands	7.6	0	0	0.4	2.8	0	10.7
Unallocated	0	0.3	-1.7	17.5	9.0	2.8	27.9
Geography							
Rescission	0	0	0	0	0	0	*-30.0*b
Total	**2,097.3**	**453.9**	**110.2**	**100.5**	**96.6**	**56.7**	**2,885.2**b

Source: NPS Budget Office, personal communication, September-November 2014.

Notes: Figures reflect a supplemental appropriation in P.L. 113-2 for Superstorm Sandy response and recovery.

The supplemental added $329.8 million to the NPS's Construction account and $47.5 million to the Historic Preservation Fund account.

The total includes allocations to the NPS from a central DOI fund for Wildland Fire Management but does not include other allocations to the NPS.

"Unallocated geography" refers to funding that was not allocated to individual states.

[a] The state of Delaware did not contain a national park unit at the start of FY2013. The President proclaimed the First State National Monument in Delaware on March 25, 2013. Operating funds were first appropriated for this park unit in FY2014.

[b] The total reflects a $30.0 million rescission of contract authority from the Land and Water Conservation Fund. Thus, the column totals for the individual appropriations accounts do not sum to the discretionary appropriations total.

Table 9. National Park Service Revenue by State, FY2013
(in millions of dollars)

	Recreation Fees[a]	Concession Franchise Fees	O&M of Quarters	Transportation Systems Fund	Park Buildings Lease and Maintenance Fund	Other[b]	Total Revenues
Alaska	1.7	4.4	1.1	0	0.3	4.3[c]	11.8
Arizona	26.9	8.3	0	0	0	0.1	35.2
Arkansas	0.5	0.2	0	0	0	<0.1	0.6
California	36.8	17.0	5.3	1.2	4.0	0.4	64.6
Colorado	8.7	1.7	9.4	13.3	<0.1	<0.1	33.1
Connecticut	<0.1	0	0	0	0	0	<0.1
Delaware	0	0	0	0	0	0	0
District of Columbia	0.5	1.1	0.5	0.2	<0.1	<0.1	2.3
Florida	5.1	1.3	0	0	0	<0.1	6.4
Georgia	1.4	0.1	1.4	0.5	0.2	0	3.7
Hawaii	7.3	0	0	0	0	<0.1	7.3
Idaho	3.0	0	0	0	0	0	3.0
Illinois	0.1	0	0	0	0	<0.1	0.1
Indiana	0.3	0	0	0	0	0	0.3
Iowa	<0.1	0	0	0	0	0	<0.1
Kansas	0	0	0	0	0	0	0
Kentucky	3.1	0.2	0	0	0	<0.1	3.2
Louisiana	0	0	0	0	0	0	0
Maine	2.8	0.6	0	0	0	0	3.3
Maryland	2.9	0.1	0	0	0	<0.1	3.0
Massachusetts	1.6	0.1	0	0	0	<0.1	1.7
Michigan	2.2	0.2	0	0	0	<0.1	2.3

	Recreation Feesa	Concession Franchise Fees	O&M of Quarters	Transportation Systems Fund	Park Buildings Lease and Maintenance Fund	Otherb	Total Revenues
Minnesota	0.1	<0.1	0	0	0	0	0.1
Mississippi	1.1	0.2	0	0	0	<0.1	1.3
Missouri	2.8	0.1	0	0	0	<0.1	2.9
Montana	9.6	0.3	0	0	0	0.9d	10.7
Nebraska	0.1	0	0.7	<0.1	0.4	0	1.2
Nevada	1.0	0.8	0	0	0	<0.1	1.8
New Hampshire	<0.1	0	0	0	0	0	<0.1
New Jersey	0.4	1.3	0	0	0	<0.1e	1.6
New Mexico	2.7	0.6	0	0	0	<0.1	3.3
New York	3.8	4.8	0	0	0	0.1	8.6
North Carolina	4.6	0.8	0	0	0	0	5.4
North Dakota	0.5	<0.1	0	0	0	0	0.5
Ohio	0.3	0	0	0	0	<0.1	0.3
Oklahoma	0.3	0	0	0	0	0	0.3
Oregon	1.6	0.4	0	0	0	0	2.0
Pennsylvania	0.3	<0.1	2.9	1.0	1.4	<0.1e	5.6
Rhode Island	<0.1	0	0	0	0	0	<0.1
South Carolina	0.1	0.7	0	0	0	0	0.8
South Dakota	2.4	1.9	0	0	0	<0.1	4.3
Tennessee	0.2	0	0	0	0	<0.1	0.2
Texas	1.7	0.2	0	0	0	<0.1	2.0
Utah	14.7	6.0	0	0	0	0.1	20.7
Vermont	<0.1	0	0	0	0	0	<0.1
Virginia	7.5	3.1	0	0	0	<0.1	10.6
Washington	6.2	1.5	0	0	0	<0.1	7.8
West Virginia	<0.1	0	0	0	0	<0.1	<0.1

Table 9. (Continued)

	Recreation Feesa	Concession Franchise Fees	O&M of Quarters	Transportation Systems Fund	Park Buildings Lease and Maintenance Fund	Otherb	Total Revenues
Wisconsin	0.1	<0.1	0	0	0	0	0.1
Wyoming	5.8	6.9	0	0	0	0.1[d]	12.8
Puerto Rico	2.2	<0.1	0	0	0	<0.1	2.2
Virgin Islands	0.7	0.1	0	0	0	<0.1	0.8
Unallocated	4.3a	0	0	0	0	39.3f	43.6
Geography							
Total	**179.5**	**64.8**	**21.3**	**16.2**	**6.3**	**45.3**	**333.4**

Source: NPS Budget Office, personal communication, September-November 2014.

Notes: In general, figures in the table reflect revenues collected and thus do not reflect sequestration. However, in the case of Recreation Fees, the amounts shown for *individual states* do reflect sequestration (see note "a"), although the total does not.

a The Recreation Fee collections shown for each individual state are reduced based on the President's March 1, 2013, sequester order. The amount of revenue that was sequestered is represented under unallocated geography, due to NPS tracking procedures. Revenues from certain sales of interagency recreation passes also are included in the unallocated geography category for Recreation Fees.

[b] Figures in this column include revenues from the Filming and Photography Special Use Fee Program, as well as any other programs specifically noted.

[c] This figure includes filming and photography fees and Glacier Bay National Park Resource Protection.

[d] The figures for Montana and Wyoming include filming and photography fees and visitor fees used for educational expenses of the children of employees at Yellowstone and for payment for tax losses on land at Grand Teton.

[e] The figures for New Jersey and Pennsylvania include fees from filming and photography and from Delaware Water Gap National Recreation Area Route 209 Operations.

[f] This figure primarily represents donations. The Park Service does not track donations by state, although some funding may be for use at a specific site depending on the terms of the donation.

Other factors influencing appropriations to each state include the extent of visitor services at its national park units; park security needs, which may be especially great in urban areas;[71] the presence of NPS regional offices in a state;[72] the number of facilities to be maintained in each park unit; and the costs of mitigating threats to natural and cultural resources, among others.

In FY2013, appropriations by state also were affected by the impact of Superstorm Sandy on many East Coast parks. Congress appropriated supplemental funding of $377.3 million for the Construction account and the Historic Preservation Fund, to be used for response to and recovery from the storm. Eastern states such as New York, where the Statue of Liberty and other assets suffered serious damage, benefited from these funds. For example, New York's share of appropriations from NPS's Construction account in FY2013 was over 60% of the account total.

Revenue

The NPS estimates its collected revenues at $333.4 million for FY2013.[73] **Table 9** shows revenues collected in each state,[74] and **Figure 6** shows revenues collected by type. The largest source of NPS revenues in FY2013 was the Recreation Fee Program, through which the agency collected $179.5 million (53.8% of the total). The second-largest source was Concession Franchise Fees, with $64.8 million (19.4%) collected. Revenues were $21.3 million (6.4%) from Operation and Maintenance of Quarters, $16.2 million (4.9%) from the Transportation Systems Fund, $6.3 million (1.9%) from the Park Buildings Lease and Maintenance Fund, and $45.3 million (13.6%) from a variety of other sources.[75] These programs are discussed further in the "Mandatory Appropriations" section.

The revenues collected in each state varied, with the highest totals in California ($64.6 million), Arizona ($35.2 million), Colorado ($33.1 million), and Utah ($20.7 million). These states contain some of the National Park System's best-known units—such as Grand Canyon National Park (AZ), Yosemite National Park (CA), Zion National Park (UT), and Rocky Mountain National Park (CO)—which receive high numbers of visitors. However, park visitation levels do not necessarily correspond with revenue collections. For example, in 2013, several of the most visited park units (such as the Lincoln Memorial in Washington, DC; Great Smoky Mountains National Park in North Carolina and Tennessee, and the Natchez Trace Parkway in Alabama, Mississippi, and Tennessee) were in states with relatively low amounts of revenues. In addition to visitor traffic, revenues also depend on whether entrance and recreation use fees are charged at a state's park units; how high the fees are; how much concessioners pay to the NPS to offer visitor services; and whether other types of fees, such as those for the use of transportation within the parks or for operation and maintenance of quarters, are collected.

Revenues collected in some states in FY2013 were affected by damages to the parks from Superstorm Sandy. Some park units were closed for long periods of time after the storm. For example, the Statue of Liberty and Ellis Island in New York were closed from the time the storm struck (on October 28, 2012) through July 4, 2013, depressing park visitation and revenues in New York during FY2013.

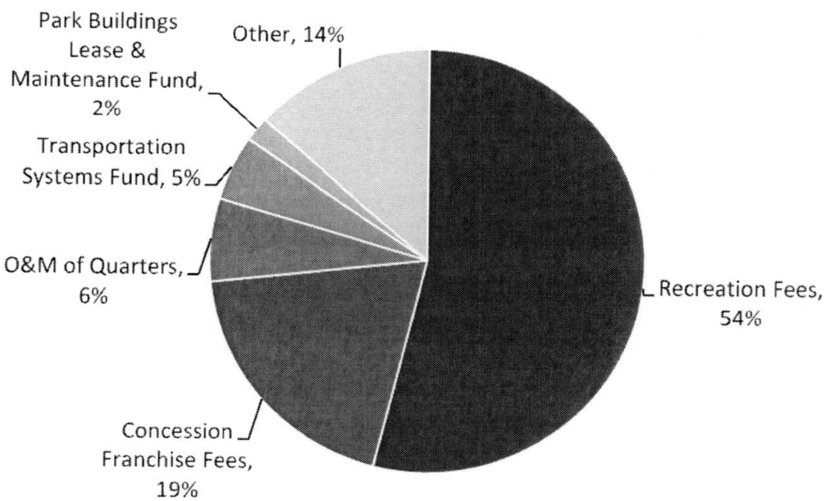

Source: Prepared by CRS with data from the NPS Budget Office, personal communication, September-November 2014.

Figure 6. National Park Service Revenue by Type, FY2013.

FOREST SERVICE

Appropriations

Appropriations data for the Forest Service (FS) are provided in this report for 12 western states: Alaska, Arizona, California, Colorado, Idaho, Montana,

Nevada, New Mexico, Oregon, Utah, Washington, and Wyoming. Those 12 western states contain 163.7 million acres (84.8%) of the total 193.0 million acres of the National Forest System. See **Table 10**.[76] These states also account for a large portion of the agency's overall appropriations.

Table 10. National Forest System Units and Acreage in 12 Western States, 2013

Western State	NFS Units	NFS Acreage
Alaska	2	22,207,400
Arizona	7	11,204,428
California	41	20,747,885
Colorado	14	14,482,727
Idaho	18	20,444,413
Montana	14	17,151,047
Nevada	4	5,759,160
New Mexico	17	9,311,527
Oregon	22	15,674,661
Utah	10	8,187,926
Washington	20	9,323,705
Wyoming	11	9,214,708
Total, 12 western states	180	163,709,587

Source: Forest Service, *Land Areas Report (LAR)-as of September 30, 2013*, Table 4, at http://www.fs.fed.us/land/staff/lar/LAR2013/lar2013index.html.

Notes: NFS Units includes national forests, national grasslands, purchase units, research areas, and other miscellaneous federal land designations managed by the Forest Service. The total of 180 units reflects double counting, because some units are in more than one state.

The FS estimates that appropriations for the 12 western states for FY2013 were $3,380.1 million. The majority of this funding was discretionary. Specifically, the total includes $2,863.2 million (84.7%) in discretionary appropriations and $516.9 million (15.3%) in mandatory appropriations. **Table 11** and **Figure 7** provide the discretionary, mandatory, and total FS appropriations for the 12 western states.

A large majority of the appropriations are used for managing the 163.7 million acres of agency-owned lands in the 12 western states. Specifically, of the total appropriations, $3,105.1 million (91.9%) was spent on agency lands, although the percentage varies by state. See **Table 12** for the percentage of total funding spent in each of the western states on federal and nonfederal land.

Discretionary Appropriations

For FY2013, the 12 western states received $2,863.2 million in discretionary appropriations through several accounts, as shown in **Table 13**. The largest account was for Wildland Fire Management, which in FY2013 received $1,696.7 million (59.3%) of FS's discretionary appropriations for the 12 western states. This account funds activities related to the management of unplanned and unwanted fires, including planning for and suppression of wildfires. The second-largest discretionary account for the 12 western states was the National Forest System, which received $647.6 million (22.6%) of the total. The National Forest System account funds an array of Forest Service programs and activities related to the management of the agency-owned lands.

The remaining FS FY2013 discretionary appropriation in the 12 western states was considerably smaller. The "Other" category totaled $214.6 million (7.5%), primarily reflecting discretionary indirect costs allocations. The Capital Improvement and Maintenance account—which funds activities related to the agency's infrastructure needs—received $212.2 million (7.4%). State and Private Forestry received $60.4 million (2.1%) for programs to provide financial and technical assistance to nonfederal forest owners and managers, and to protect communities and the environment from insects, diseases, and invasive plants. The 12 western states received $31.1 million (1.1%) for Land Acquisition and $0.6 million (<0.1%) for Forest and Rangeland Research.

Mandatory Appropriations

The FS has over 20 permanent appropriations accounts and several trust funds that constitute mandatory spending. In this report, these accounts and trust funds have been combined into broad categories representing trust funds, permanent appropriations, payment to states, and other mandatory appropriations, as shown in **Table 14**.

The budget authority for these accounts is provided for in various authorizing laws. For several of these accounts, the budget authority is dependent on the level of receipts received for specific National Forest System activities, and some have geographic or programmatic expenditure restrictions. Of the $516.9 million provided in mandatory appropriations, the largest amount was from the Payment to States fund, $231.9 million (44.9%), which includes the payments authorized under SRS and the various revenue-sharing payments.

The second-largest category of mandatory appropriations, with $146.6 million (28.4%), was for various permanent funds, such as the Brush Disposal

Fund, and the collection of cost recovery fees for administering right-of-way authorizations, among others.

FS trust funds, such as those used for cooperative work agreements, timber sale deposits, and reforestation projects, accounted for $97.6 million, 18.9% of the total. Indirect costs associated with the mandatory accounts were $40.8 million, 7.9% of the total appropriation.

Discussion

A precise total of FS appropriations for each state is difficult to ascertain; therefore the figures provided are considered estimates. In fact, the FS tracks and reports very little data by state. This is due in part to the agency's regional organization, which does not follow state boundaries. Rather, an FS region may contain portions of several states. Region 4, for example, contains the national forests located in Nevada, Utah, and portions of Idaho and Wyoming.[77]

In addition, national forests may cross state boundaries. For example, 22 western national forests are located in more than one state.[78] Further, the agency's appropriations accounts are allocated at both the regional and national levels. For instance, FS appropriations for the National Forest System (NFS) account, among others, are allocated to nine FS regions.[79] Other appropriations—such as for suppression operations within the Wildland Fire Management subaccount—are appropriated to the national office to be allocated on an as-needed basis. While it may seem feasible to apportion funding based on national forest acreage, there is not always a one-to-one distribution between dollars and forest acreage.[80]

The 12 western states received widely varying amounts of FY2013 appropriations, ranging from $64.3 million for Nevada to $984.1 million for California. The level of appropriations in each state is influenced by a number of factors.

One is the amount of lands managed by the FS in each state, which varies from 5.8 million acres in Nevada to 22.2 million acres in Alaska. Different land resources, conditions, uses, and impacts can affect the cost of land management, as can demographics. In addition, wildfire activity varies from state to state, contributing to differences in appropriations for wildland fire management among states.

Table 11. Forest Service Appropriations for 12 Western States, FY2013 (in millions of dollars)

	Discretionary Appropriations	Mandatory Appropriationsa	Total Appropriations
Alaska	95.0	27.3	122.3
Arizona	147.8	27.7	175.5
California	851.5	132.6	984.1
Colorado	190.0	29.7	219.7
Idaho	319.0	51.8	370.8
Montana	277.0	35.6	312.5
Nevada	58.9	5.4	64.3
New Mexico	197.0	24.6	221.6
Oregon	362.8	127.1	489.9
Utah	130.2	20.3	150.5
Washington	171.3	26.6	197.9
Wyoming	62.7	8.2	70.9
Total, 12 western states	**2,863.2**	**516.9**	**3,380.1**
Total, Forest Service	**4,934.7**	**775.1**	**5,709.8**

Source: Data on the 12 western states provided by Forest Service, Budget Office, September 2014. Total Forest Service discretionary appropriations data are derived from detailed funding tables prepared by the House Committee on Appropriations. Total mandatory appropriations data are derived from Forest Service, *Fiscal Year 2015 Budget Justification*, at http://www.fs.fed.us/sites /default/files/media/2014/25/2015-BudgetJustification030614.pdf. Adapted by CRS.

Notes:

a. Forest Service data on mandatory appropriations in the 12 western states reflect new budget authority for FY2013 but may also reflect program level data for FY2013, meaning that some carry-over funds may have been included. The $775.1 million figure shown for the total mandatory appropriation reflects new FY2013 budget authority. The total program level for FY2013 mandatory appropriations was $812.6 million.

Table 12. Percent of Forest Service Spending on Federal Lands and Nonfederal Lands in 12 Western States

	Federal Land Spending	Nonfederal Land Spending
Alaska	86.0%	14.0%
Arizona	92.6%	7.4%
California	96.4%	3.6%
Colorado	90.1%	9.9%
Idaho	93.2%	6.8%

	Federal Land Spending	Nonfederal Land Spending
Montana	89.3%	10.7%
Nevada	92.3%	7.7%
New Mexico	93.5%	6.5%
Oregon	85.2%	14.8%
Utah	87.6%	12.4%
Washington	94.5%	5.5%
Wyoming	90.0%	10.0%
Overall, 12 western states	**91.9%**	**8.1%**

Source: Data provided by the Forest Service, Budget Office, September 2014. Adapted by CRS.

Notes: Nonfederal land spending refers to appropriations for the Forest Service's various technical and financial assistance programs for nonfederal forest landowners, as well as certain Payments to States monies.

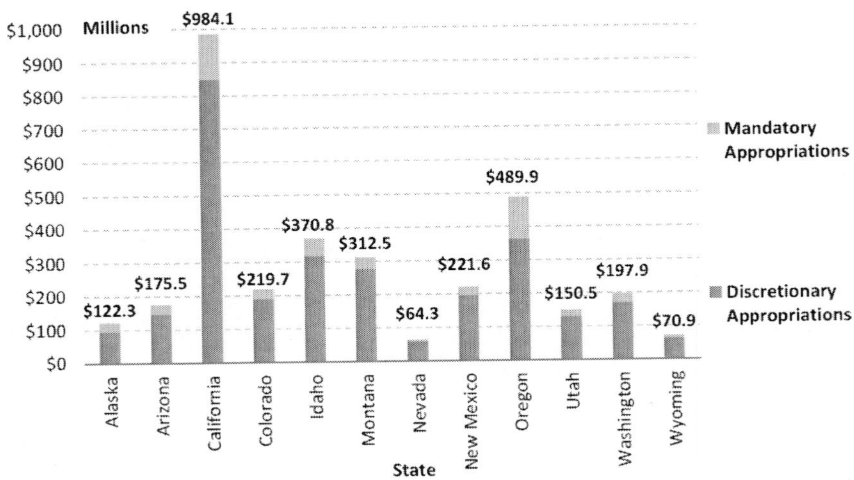

Source: Prepared by CRS with data from the Forest Service, Budget Office, September 2014.

Notes: Forest Service data on mandatory appropriations in the 12 western states reflect new budget authority for FY2013 but may also reflect program level data for FY2013, meaning that some carry-over funds may have been included.

Figure 7. Forest Service Appropriations for 12 Western States, FY2013.

Table 13. Forest Service Discretionary Appropriations for 12 Western States, FY2013; (in millions of dollars)

	Wildland Fire Management[a]	National Forest System	Capital Improvement and Maintenance	State and Private Forestry	Land Acquisition[b]	Forest and Rangeland Research	Other[c]	Total Discretionary Appropriations
Alaska	21.6	39.2	14.2	3.8	0.7	0.3	15.4	95.0
Arizona	74.1	44.4	13.6	<0.1	0.3	<0.1	15.6	147.8
California	660.2	121.3	50.8	3.3	1.0	<0.1	14.8	851.5
Colorado	101.6	45.9	17.5	7.9	<0.1	<0.1	16.9	190.0
Idaho	201.4	69.0	20.4	0.9	6.0	0	21.3	319.0
Montana	128.1	72.8	19.4	12.7	16.9	0	27.1	277.0
Nevada	43.2	8.2	2.2	1.5	0	0	3.7	58.9
New Mexico	109.2	51.9	10.9	5.0	0.5	0	19.6	197.0
Oregon	196.3	90.2	27.1	10.4	2.5	0.2	36.0	362.8
Utah	56.4	41.6	10.3	5.9	1.3	<0.1	14.6	130.2
Washington	81.7	43.5	18.1	5.3	1.1	0.1	21.4	171.3
Wyoming	22.9	19.5	7.4	3.9	1.0	0	8.0	62.7
Total, 12 western states	**1,696.7**	**647.6**	**212.2**	**60.4**	**31.1**	**0.6**	**214.6**	**2,863.2**

Source: Data provided by the Forest Service, Budget Office, September 2014. Adapted by CRS.

Notes:

[a] Transfers from the FLAME Wildfire Suppression Reserve Fund are included in the Wildland Fire Management figures in this column. The FLAME account, funded through discretionary appropriations, functions as a reserve where funds may be transferred to the Wildland Fire Management account in certain situations to support wildfire suppression operations.

[b] Figures in this column reflect appropriations for the Forest Service Land Acquisition account as well as several smaller accounts related to land acquisition, such as for special acts acquisitions and land exchanges.

[c] Figures in this column primarily reflect indirect costs for various administrative expenses that are not directly chargeable to one specific program, project, or activity. These funds are appropriated through various discretionary accounts. The figures also include discretionary appropriations for the relatively smaller Forest Service accounts not reported in other columns in this table.

Table 14. Forest Service Mandatory Appropriations for 12 Western States, FY2013 (in millions of dollars)

	Payment to States	Permanent Accounts	Trust Funds	Indirect Costsa	Total Mandatory Appropriation
Alaska	13.6	7.3	2.4	4.0	27.3
Arizona	16.3	7.3	1.3	2.9	27.7
California	38.7	43.0	48.7	2.3	132.6
Colorado	14.0	9.7	3.4	2.6	29.7
Idaho	28.6	15.5	4.3	3.5	51.8
Montana	21.1	6.6	4.4	3.5	35.6
Nevada	4.3	0.7	0	0.3	5.4
New Mexico	11.7	6.8	3.6	2.4	24.6
Oregon	66.6	27.0	20.9	12.6	127.1
Utah	10.8	5.4	1.9	2.3	20.3
Washington	4.1	13.9	5.2	3.3	26.6
Wyoming	2.2	3.4	1.6	1.0	8.2
Total, 12 western states	**231.9**	**146.6**	**97.6**	**40.8**	**516.9**

Source: Data provided by the Forest Service, Budget Office, September 2014. Adapted by CRS. The figures reflect new FY2013 budget authority but may also reflect program level data for FY2013, meaning that some carry-over funds may have been included.

Notes:

[a] Indirect costs reflect various administrative expenses that are not directly chargeable to one specific program, project, or activity but are appropriated through various mandatory accounts.

Revenue

Revenue collected by the Forest Service in FY2013 totaled $223.6 million. These monies were derived from a variety of activities and resources from National Forest System land. **Table 15** shows the amount of revenue by state from each source during FY2013, and **Figure 8** shows revenue by type.

Recreation generated the most revenue from the national forest lands—$61.4 million (27.5%) of the total. KV revenue—collections authorized under the Knutson-Vandenberg Act of June 9, 1930[81]—was the second-largest source of revenue, generating $49.4 million (22.1%). Timber sales accounted for the third-largest source, generating $32.0 million (14.3%), while salvage timber sales produced an additional $28.6 million (12.8%). In addition, miscellaneous other deposits or credits associated with timber sales, such as road credits or deposits into the Timber Sale Pipeline Restoration Fund, brought in $19.6 million (8.7%).[82] Land-use activities accounted for $18.0 million (8.0%), and power-generating activities or projects on National Forest System land generated $8.0 million (3.6%). Other sources of revenue were grazing permit fees ($4.8 million, 2.2%) and certain mineral sales ($1.9 million, 0.8%). As shown in **Table 15**, the national forest revenue generated varies widely by state, ranging from just over $200 in North Dakota to $37.5 million in California. Among the 12 western states, Alaska generated the least amount of revenue, at $1.6 million. The variability is due to several factors, including the amount of National Forest System land in each state and the types of resources contained on those lands. For example, forest type and age, as well as topography, influence the potential amount and value of timber sales. Similarly, the kinds of land uses, such as recreation and power right-of-ways; the frequency and extent of these uses; as well as the value of the land in general influence collections. Other factors, such as proximity to population centers, also contribute to certain revenue sources. For example, recreation generated the most revenue in both California and Colorado national forests, due in part to the close location of several national forests within both of those states to large metropolitan areas.

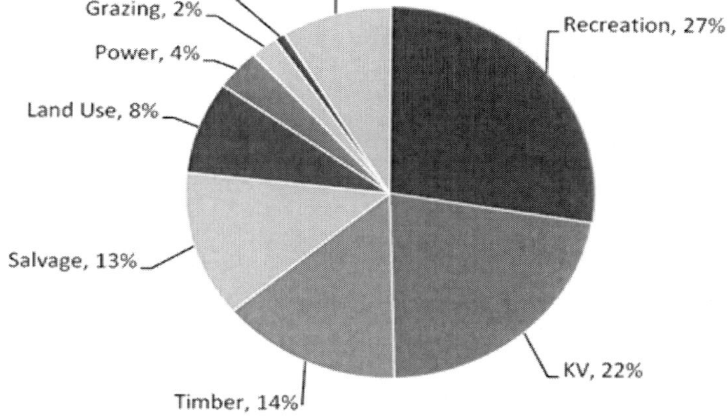

Source: Prepared by CRS with data from: U.S. Department of Agriculture, Forest Service, *All Service Receipts (ASR), Final Forest Statement of Receipts (ASR-13-2)*, http://www.fs.usda.gov/Internet/FSE_DOCUMENTS/ stelprd3795423.pdf.

Figure 8. Forest Service Revenue by Type, FY2013.

Table 15. Forest Service Revenue by State, FY2013 (in millions of dollars)

	Recreation	KV	Timber	Salvage	Land Use	Power	Grazing	Minerals	Other	Total
Alabama	<0.1	1.5	0.6	<0.1	<0.1	<0.1	0	0	0	2.1
Alaska	0.1	<0.1	0.4	0.2	0.4	0.1	0	0.4	0	1.6
Arizona	1.5	0.1	0.1	0.4	1.1	0.4	0.8	0.3	0	4.7
Arkansas	0.1	5.4	2.6	0.2	0.4	<0.1	<0.1	<0.1	2.9	11.6
California	16.1	2.7	2.3	3.5	7.1	4.8	0.3	-0.3	0.9	37.5
Colorado	17.6	0.8	0.9	0.8	1.6	0.1	0.6	<0.1	<0.1	22.5
Connecticut	0	0	0	0	0	0	0	0	0	0
Delaware	0	0	0	0	0	0	0	0	0	0
Florida	0.4	1.3	0.2	0.4	0.5	0.1	0	0	<0.1	2.9
Georgia	<0.1	0.2	0.1	<0.1	0.1	<0.1	0	0	0.1	0.6
Hawaii	0	0	0	0	0	0	0	0	0	0
Idaho	2.1	1.4	0.3	2.5	0.6	0.2	0.6	<0.1	0.9	8.6
Illinois	0	0	<0.1	0	0.8	<0.1	0	<0.1	0	0.8
Indiana	<0.1	0.1	<0.1	<0.1	<0.1	<0.1	0	0	0	0.1
Iowa	0	0	0	0	0	0	0	0	0	0
Kansas	0	0	0	0	0	0	0	0	0	0
Kentucky	<0.1	0.2	0.1	<0.1	0.1	0.1	<0.1	<0.1	<0.1	0.6
Louisiana	<0.1	3.4	2.5	<0.1	0.1	0.1	<0.1	<0.1	0.4	6.5
Maine	<0.1	<0.1	<0.1	<0.1	<0.1	<0.1	0	<0.1	<0.1	0.1
Maryland	0	0	0	0	0	0	0	0	0	0
Massachusetts	0	0	0	0	0	0	0	0	0	0
Michigan	0.4	2.9	3.2	2.2	0.3	0.1	0	<0.1	2.4	11.5

Table 15. (Continued)

	Recreation	KV	Timber	Salvage	Land Use	Power	Grazing	Minerals	Other	Total
Minnesota	1.5	1.6	0.2	1.1	0.1	<0.1	0	0.3	0.2	5.0
Mississippi	0	2.3	0.7	0.2	0.1	0.1	<0.1	0	0.8	4.1
Missouri	0	1.0	0.2	1.6	0.1	<0.1	<0.1	0	0.5	3.4
Montana	2.7	1.4	0.2	2.6	0.4	0.2	0.4	<0.1	0.1	8.1
Nebraska	0	<0.1	<0.1	0	<0.1	0	<0.1	0	0	0.1
Nevada	1.0	0	<0.1	<0.1	0.5	<0.1	0.2	0	0	1.8
New Hampshire	0.6	0.2	0.2	0.5	<0.1	<0.1	0	<0.1	0.2	1.7
New Jersey	0	0	0	0	0	0	0	0	0	0
New Mexico	0.7	0.1	0.1	0.3	0.7	<0.1	0.5	<0.1	0.1	2.7
New York	0	0	<0.1	<0.1	<0.1	<0.1	0	0	0	<0.1
North Carolina	0.1	0.8	0.3	0.1	0.3	0.2	0	<0.1	0.2	1.8
North Dakota	<0.1	0	<0.1	<0.1	<0.1	<0.1	<0.1	0	0	<0.1
Ohio	<0.1	0.1	0.1	0	0.1	<0.1	0	0	0.1	0.3
Oklahoma	0	0.8	0.5	<0.1	<0.1	0	<0.1	<0.1	0.5	1.8
Oregon	5.5	10.1	10.3	5.8	0.8	0.3	0.4	<0.1	3.0	36.2
Pennsylvania	0.1	2.0	1.8	0.7	0.1	<0.1	<0.1	0	2.2	6.9
Rhode Island	0	0	0	0	0	0	0	0	0	0
South Carolina	<0.1	2.1	1.5	0.1	0.1	0	<0.1	0	0.7	4.5
South Dakota	0.2	2.0	0.1	0.2	0.1	0.1	0.1	<0.1	0.5	3.3
Tennessee	0.3	0.1	<0.1	<0.1	0.2	<0.1	0	<0.1	0.1	0.7
Texas	<0.1	0.2	0.5	0.2	0.2	<0.1	0	0	0.3	1.3
Utah	1.9	0.1	0.1	0.5	0.3	0.4	0.5	<0.1	0.1	3.9
Vermont	0.5	<0.1	<0.1	0.1	<0.1	<0.1	0	0	<0.1	0.8

	Recreation	KV	Timber	Salvage	Land Use	Power	Grazing	Minerals	Other	Total
Virginia	0	0.6	0.1	0.1	0.1	0.1	<0.1	<0.1	0.2	1.1
Washington	3.6	1.1	0.4	2.4	0.4	0.1	0.1	<0.1	0.5	8.7
West Virginia	0	0.5	0.4	<0.1	0.1	<0.1	<0.1	<0.1	0.4	1.4
Wisconsin	0.1	1.6	1.1	1.1	<0.1	0.1	0	0	1.0	5.1
Wyoming	4.2	0.6	0.1	0.4	0.2	0.1	0.3	1.0	0.1	7.0
Puerto Rico	0	0	0	0	0	0	0	0	0	0
Total	61.4	49.4	32.0	28.6	18.0	8.0	4.8	1.9	19.6	223.6

Source: U.S. Department of Agriculture, Forest Service, *All Service Receipts (ASR), Final Forest Statement of Receipts (ASR-13-2)*, http://www.fs.usda.gov/Internet/FSE_DOCUMENTS/stelprd3795423.pdf.

Notes: Nine states do not contain any national forest land: Connecticut, Delaware, Hawaii, Iowa, Kansas, Maryland, Massachusetts, New Jersey, and Rhode Island. Recreation revenue is amounts collected for all types of recreation, including user fees collected under the Land and Water Conservation Fund. KV revenue is collections authorized under the Knutson-Vandenberg Act of June 9, 1930, from timber sale purchasers for sale area improvement work and reforestation. Timber revenue is amounts collected for the sale of timber and certain other forest products. Salvage sale revenue is derived from payments for salvageable material used to facilitate the timely removal of damaged timber. Land use revenue is amounts collected for land uses except power, minerals, or recreational uses. Power revenue is amounts collected for uses authorized by FS permits or easements for all types of power-generating projects and power transmission line rights-of-way. Grazing revenue is amounts collected for grazing fees in the national forests, with both the eastern and western grazing fees combined. Minerals revenue is amounts collected from the sale of minerals (including quartz crystals) and permit fees. Includes mineral lease and permit fees collected by DOI on acquired lands having National Forest status but does not include any mineral revenue derived from National Forest System land which was established from the public domain. Other revenue includes road credits and deposits made by timber sale contract purchasers, and deposits to the Timber Sale Pipeline Restoration Fund, which is derived from certain timber sale revenues.

DISTRIBUTIONS FROM FEDERAL HIGHWAY ADMINISTRATION

The BLM, FWS, NPS, and FS receive distributions of funds from other agencies for several purposes. A major program is the distribution of Federal Highway Administration (FHWA) funds to states for federal lands projects. FHWA and its predecessor offices and agencies have been involved in the development of roads to and through federal lands since 1905.[83] The distribution of federal lands highway funds for FY2013 and FY2014 was authorized by the Moving Ahead for Progress in the 21st Century Act (MAP-21)[84] and extended through May 31, 2015, by the Highway and Transportation Funding Act of 2014.[85] MAP-21 made major changes to federal lands and tribal transportation programs.[86]

The Federal Lands Highway Program is administered by FHWA's Office of Federal Lands Highway. As restructured by MAP-21, it has three components: the Federal Lands Transportation Program (FLTP), the Federal Lands Access Program (FLAP), and the Federal Lands Planning Program (FLPP).[87] FLTP primarily funds transportation facilities on federal lands, whereas FLAP primarily funds transportation facilities that provide access to federal lands. FLPP provides funds to carry out transportation planning for federal lands and tribal transportation facilities.

MAP-21 authorized $300 million for FLTP and $250 million for FLAP for FY2013. FLPP receives a maximum 5% set-aside from these two programs. According to MAP-21, $240 million of FLTP funds goes to NPS, $30 million to FWS, and the remaining $30 million is allocated competitively among BLM, FS, and the U.S. Army Corps of Engineers. In addition to the planning set-aside, these amounts are subject to other reductions, such as an obligation limitation.[88] FLTP funds are distributed among the states according to agency priorities. Authorized FLAP funds are also subject to an obligation limitation. Available FLAP funds are distributed by formula. Eighty percent of FLAP funds go to states that contain at least 1.5% of the national total of federal lands, and the remaining 20% go to states with less than 1.5% of the national total.[89] Funds within these two groups are then distributed to individual states based on four factors: (1) 55% according to a state's share of federal public road miles; (2) 30% according to a state's share of recreational visitation; (3) 10% according to a state's share of federal public bridges; and (4) 5% according to a state's share of federal land area.

In addition to funds for FLTP, FLAP, and FLPP, the Office of Federal Lands Highway also distributed funding from two other federal lands highway programs in FY2013. One involved the remaining FY2012 funding from the Public Lands Highway Discretionary Program, a program authorized under the Safe, Accountable, Flexible, Efficient Transportation Equity Act: A Legacy for Users.[90] The other was funding approved for FY2013 disasters under the Emergency Relief for Federally Owned Roads Program (ERFO).[91]

In FY2013, $573.8 million was distributed by Federal Lands Highway[92] from these five programs to BLM, FWS, NPS, or FS, or to a state Programming Decisions Committee (PDC).[93] Almost half of the funds available ($280.6 million, 48.9%) went to NPS, and another two-fifths ($227.2 million, 39.6%) went to state PDCs. The remaining funds were allocated to FWS (6.4%), FS (3.5%), and BLM (1.7%). Of the $573.8 million, $82.9 million cannot be identified by state because it was attributed only to a federal land management agency ($65.0 million) or it was unallocated in FY2013 ($18.0 million). The distribution by state and agency of the remaining $490.8 million can be seen in Table 16. Figure 9 shows the distribution by agency.

Table 16. Federal Highway Administration Distributions for Federal Lands, by Agency and State, FY2013 (in millions of dollars)

State	NPS	State PDC	FWS	FS	BLM	Total
Alabama	2.6	1.0	0	0	0	3.6
Alaska	6.1	7.1	1.5	0.7	0	15.4
Arizona	10.7	13.5	0	0	0	24.3
Arkansas	<0.1	3.1	0	0	0	3.2
California	48.9	35.7	1.5	<0.1	0.3	86.5
Colorado	7.8	16.7	2.1	0.4	0.2	27.1
Connecticut	0	<0.1	0	0	0	<0.1
Delaware	0	<0.1	<0.1	0	0	<0.1
District of Columbia	5.6	1.3	0	0	0	6.9
Florida	0.2	2.0	0.8	0	0	3.0
Georgia	0.4	2.3	0.1	0	0	2.8
Hawaii	0.2	0.3	0	0	0	0.4
Idaho	1.1	17.1	0	0	<0.1	18.2
Illinois	0	0.9	0	0	0	0.9
Indiana	<0.1	0.5	0	0	0	0.5
Iowa	0	0.3	2.8	0	0	3.1
Kansas	0.6	0.8	2.2	0	0	3.6
Kentucky	<0.1	1.6	0	0	0	1.7

Table 16. (Continued)

State	NPS	State PDC	FWS	FS	BLM	Total
Louisiana	0	1.3	2.2	0	0	3.5
Maine	0	0.3	0	0	0	0.3
Maryland	3.8	0.5	0.2	0	0	4.5
Massachusetts	<0.1	0.4	0.1	0	0	0.5
Michigan	0.1	1.6	0.8	0	0	2.5
Minnesota	0.5	1.3	0.3	0	0	2.1
Mississippi	10.1	2.9	<0.1	0	0	13.0
Missouri	<0.1	1.5	0.2	0	0	1.7
Montana	13.3	22.8	<0.1	<0.1	<0.1	36.1
Nebraska	0	0.3	<0.1	0	0	0.3
Nevada	2.8	7.1	0	0	0	9.8
New Hampshire	0	0.3	0.1	0	0	0.4
New Jersey	6.2	0.2	0.9	0	0	7.3
New Mexico	3.9	5.8	1.7	0	0	11.4
New York	24.9	0.4	<0.1	0	0	25.4
North Carolina	30.3	2.6	0	0	0	32.8
North Dakota	5.5	0.9	1.2	0	0	7.6
Ohio	1.2	0.8	0.1	0	0	2.1
Oklahoma	0.1	1.3	0	0	0	1.4
Oregon	0.6	22.1	<0.1	0.5	<0.1	23.2
Pennsylvania	0.3	1.1	0	0	0	1.4
Rhode Island	0	<0.1	0.8	0	0	0.8
South Carolina	<0.1	1.2	0.1	0	0	1.3
South Dakota	3.1	1.2	<0.1	0	0	4.2
Tennessee	4.9	2.4	0.3	0	0	7.6
Texas	0.2	2.7	4.1	0	0	6.9
Utah	0.2	10.8	0	0	1.5	12.4
Vermont	0	0.2	0.1	0	0	0.3
Virginia	18.3	3.0	2.2	0.2	<0.1	23.8
Washington	12.4	14.0	0.8	1.1	<0.1	28.2
West Virginia	0.1	1.1	<0.1	0	0	1.2
Wisconsin	0	1.8	<0.1	0	0	1.8
Wyoming	4.3	9.3	0.1	0	0	13.7
Agency	46.9	0	9.2	4.6	4.3	65.0
Unallocated	2.5	0	<0.1	12.2	3.3	18.0
Total	280.6	227.2	36.5	19.8	9.6	573.8

Source: Data prepared for CRS by the Federal Highway Administration, March 28, 2014.

Notes: PDC refers to a state Programming Decisions Committee. "Agency" represents federal lands highway funds transferred to an agency that FHWA cannot identify by place of expenditure. "Unallocated" is funding available to a land management agency in FY2013 but not allocated. These funds are likely to be allocated in FY2014.

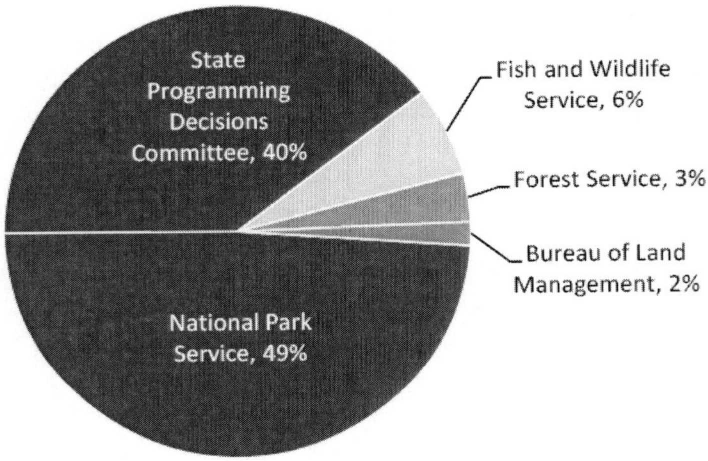

Source: Prepared by CRS with data from the Federal Highway Administration, March 28, 2014.

Figure 9. Federal Highway Administration Distributions for Federal Lands by Agency, FY2013.

PAYMENT PROGRAMS

Federally owned lands cannot be taxed but may create demand for services, such as fire protection, police cooperation, or longer roads to skirt the federal property. Under federal law, local governments are compensated through various programs due to the presence of most federally owned land. Some of these programs are run by specific agencies and apply only to one agency's land, while others are broader and apply to lands of multiple agencies.[94]

Payments in Lieu of Taxes

The Payments in Lieu of Taxes program, or PILT, [95] is the most widely applicable program and applies to many types of federally owned land. The program is administered by DOI. Under the statute, eligible lands are those in the National Park System; National Forest System; Bureau of Land Management; the National Wildlife Refuge System for land withdrawn from the public domain; lands dedicated to the use of federal water resources development projects; dredge disposal areas under the jurisdiction of the U.S. Army Corps of Engineers; lands located in the vicinity of Purgatory River Canyon and Piñon Canyon, CO, that were acquired after December 31, 1981, to expand the Fort Carson military reservation; lands on which are located semi-active or inactive Army installations used for mobilization and for reserve component training; and certain lands acquired by DOI or the Department of Agriculture under the Southern Nevada Public Land Management Act.

No precise dollar figure can be given in advance for each year's authorized level of PILT payments. Rather, the authorized level of PILT payments is calculated under a complex formula. Five factors affect the calculation of a payment to a given county: the number of acres eligible for PILT payments, the county's population, payments in prior years from other specified federal land payment programs, state laws directing payments to a particular government purpose, and the Consumer Price Index as calculated by the Bureau of Labor Statistics. According to the FY2013 *National Summary*, there were 2,130 counties eligible for PILT payments in that fiscal year.[96] Many of these counties are rural counties, which are sparsely populated. The average payment per county was $187,900. Some counties received no payment because they have very few federal lands, and PILT makes no payments under $100. By contrast, many received over $1 million, and 16 counties received over $3 million.[97] The total PILT payment in FY2013 was $401.8 million. **Table 17** shows the FY2013 payments by state. PILT payments were mandatory spending in FY2013.[98] **Figure 10** shows the combined payments to states under PILT and FS Payments to States.

Table 17. Payments in Lieu of Taxes (PILT) by State, FY2013 (in millions of dollars)

State	Payment
Alabama	0.9
Alaska	26.4
Arizona	32.2
Arkansas	5.8
California	41.4
Colorado	32.0
Connecticut	<0.1
Delaware	<0.1
District of Columbia	<0.1

State	Payment
Florida	5.0
Georgia	2.3
Hawaii	0.3
Idaho	26.3
Illinois	1.1
Indiana	0.5
Iowa	0.5
Kansas	1.1
Kentucky	1.9
Louisiana	0.6
Maine	0.3
Maryland	0.1
Massachusetts	0.1
Michigan	4.2
Minnesota	2.0
Mississippi	1.6
Missouri	3.1
Montana	26.5
Nebraska	1.1
Nevada	23.3
New Hampshire	1.8
New Jersey	0.1
New Mexico	34.7
New York	0.1
North Carolina	4.0
North Dakota	1.4
Ohio	0.6
Oklahoma	2.8
Oregon	15.6
Pennsylvania	0.7
Rhode Island	0
South Carolina	0.5
South Dakota	5.7
Tennessee	1.9
Texas	4.8
Utah	35.4
Vermont	0.9
Virginia	3.3
Washington	17.2
West Virginia	2.9
Wisconsin	1.3
Wyoming	25.3

Table 17. (Continued)

State	Payment
Guam	<0.1
Puerto Rico	<0.1
Virgin Islands	<0.1
Total	401.8

Source: DOI online summary at http://www.doi.gov/pilt/state-payments.cfm?fiscal_yr=2013&as_sfid=AAAAAAW3ubwRNC4HsGKBi0xPKX5Ji5ofcV4aIr7TN10MoovV8rZF2iK r4lqiLMWk5Hks2GpxQ%2FFU%2FFtDEw%2FopcR3X%2FblQdAJJQm0KDbG3msW0cAZ6Q%3D%3D&as_fid=r PL7JSighXU1%2FW5asmAJ.

Note: Online summary tables show a discrepancy with the FY2013 National Summary for Colorado and North Carolina, resulting in a difference in the national total shown in these sources. According to DOI officials, there were reporting errors from the two states in FY2013, leading to adjustments in the payments. The amounts shown here, from the online summary tables, are current. (Personal communication between CRS and DOI, September 12, 2014.)

Forest Service Payments to States

Counties with national forest lands and with certain BLM lands have historically received a percentage of agency revenues, primarily from timber sales. However, starting in the 1990s, timber sales declined substantially—by more than 90% in some areas from peak harvest levels in the 1980s. Thus, Congress enacted the Secure Rural Schools and Community Self-Determination Act of 2000 (SRS)[99] as a temporary, optional program of payments based in part on historic rather than current revenues.[100] For the FY2013 payment, counties had the option of receiving either a revenue-sharing payment or an SRS payment. The payments are made to states and then passed on to the counties or eligible local government units.[101]

The total FY2013 payment was $312.5 million. The vast majority of the counties opted to receive an SRS payment, which was $295.3 million or 94.5% of the total payment. However, some counties elected to receive their portion of the $17.2 million revenue-sharing payment. Oregon received the highest payment in FY2013—$97.1 million—including a $36.3 million SRS payment for the O&C lands managed by the BLM. California ($32.7 million) and Idaho ($25.2 million) received the next highest payments. Several factors influence the amount of the SRS payment, including amount of land, historical revenue level, and per capita income, while the revenue-sharing payment is set at 25% of the revenue generated on the national forest lands within the specified county. Table 18 shows each state's total payment and the portions that were from revenue sharing and SRS. Figure 10 shows the combined payments to states under PILT and FS Payments to States.

Table 18. FS Revenue-Sharing and SRS Title I and Title II Payments by State, FY2013 (in millions of dollars)

	Revenue Sharing	SRS	Total Payment
Alabama	0	1.7	1.7
Alaska	0	12.2	12.2
Arizona	0	13.0	13.0
Arkansas	0.3	6.1	6.4
California	3.9	28.8	32.7
Colorado	2.9	9.6	12.5
Connecticut	0	0	0
Delaware	0	0	0
Florida	<0.1	2.3	2.3
Georgia	<0.1	1.5	1.5
Hawaii	0	0	0
Idaho	0	25.2	25.2
Illinois	0.2	<0.1	0.3
Indiana	0	0.3	0.3
Iowa	0	0	0
Kansas	0	0	0
Kentucky	0	1.7	1.7
Louisiana	0	1.6	1.6
Maine	0	0.1	0.1
Maryland	0	0	0
Massachusetts	0	0	0
Michigan	0.7	2.9	3.6
Minnesotaa	6.2	2.2	8.4
Mississippi	0	5.3	5.3
Missouri	0	3.3	3.3
Montana	0.1	18.6	18.7
Nebraska	0	0.2	0.2
Nevada	<0.1	3.5	3.5
New Hampshire	0.3	0.2	0.5
New Jersey	0	0	0
New Mexico	0	9.5	9.5
New York	0	<0.1	<0.1

Table 18. (Continued)

	Revenue Sharing	SRS	Total Payment
North Carolina	<0.1	1.8	1.8
North Dakota	0	<0.1	<0.1
Ohio	<0.1	0.2	0.3
Oklahoma	0	0.9	0.9
Oregonb	0.1	97.0	97.1
Pennsylvania	1.9	1.0	2.9
Rhode Island	0	0	0
South Carolina	0	1.7	1.7
South Dakota	0	1.7	1.7
Tennessee	0	1.1	1.1
Texas	0	2.3	2.3
Utah	0.1	9.9	10.0
Vermont	0	0.3	0.3
Virginia	0.1	1.5	1.5
Washington	<0.1	19.0	19.0
West Virginia	0	1.7	1.7
Wisconsin	<0.1	1.7	1.7
Wyoming	0.4	3.8	4.2
Puerto Rico	0	0.1	0.1
Total	**17.2**	**295.3**	**312.5**

Source: Data compiled from personal communication between CRS and the Forest Service Legislative Affairs staff, reports available on the Forest Service Payments and Receipts at http://www.fs.usda.gov/main/pts/securepayments/projected payments; and U.S. Dept. of the Interior, Bureau of Land Management, *Official 2013 Payments*, at http://www.blm.gov/or/rac/ctypaypayments.php.

Notes: The SRS payment only includes the SRS Title I and Title III payments, and does not include amounts paid in Title II, which are to be used by the agency for projects within that county.

Nine states do not contain any national forest land and therefore do not receive any payments. This is the case for Connecticut, Delaware, Hawaii, Iowa, Kansas, Maryland, Massachusetts, New Jersey, and Rhode Island.

[a] As authorized by the Thye-Blatnick Act of June 22, 1948 (16 U.S.C. §577g), certain counties in Minnesota receive an annual payment of $6.15 million.

[b] The Oregon SRS payment includes $36.3 million paid to the O&C counties under SRS Title I and Title III.

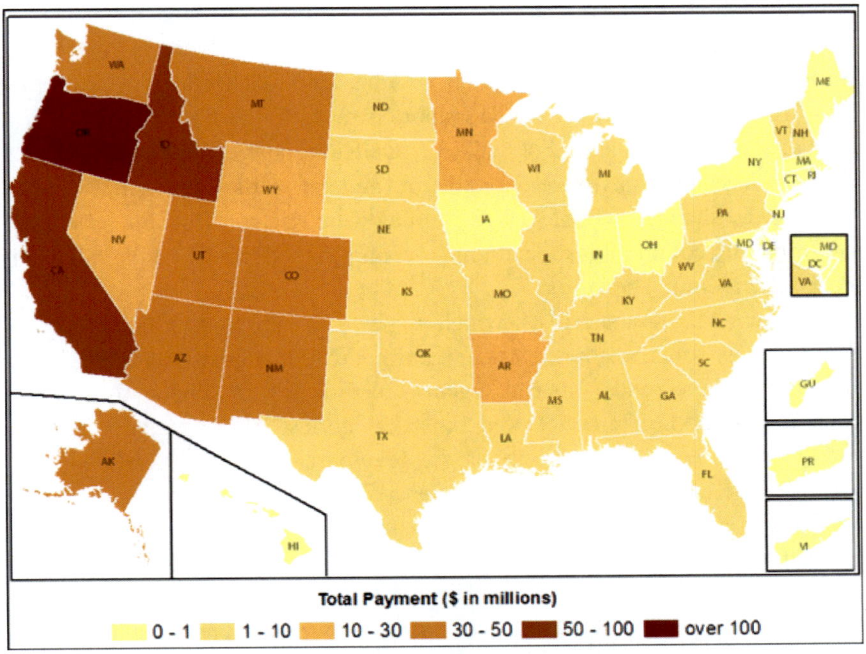

Source: Prepared by CRS from data reported in Table 17 and Table 18. See sources listed for those tables.

Notes: The Forest Service Payments to States include the revenue-sharing payment, FS SRS Title I and Title III payments, and BLM SRS Title I and Title III payments.

Figure 10. PILT and Forest Service Payments to States, FY2013.

OFFICE OF NATURAL RESOURCES REVENUE

The DOI Office of Natural Resources Revenue (ONRR) is responsible for public revenue derived from a variety of energy and mineral projects on federal lands. On a nationwide basis, ONRR reports collecting the following payments:

- bonuses to secure a lease;[102]
- rents to maintain access to leased tracts;[103] and
- royalties based on extraction volumes, among other values.[104]

The ONRR mission differs significantly from those of the federal land management agencies featured in this report. With a workforce comprised of approximately 600 accountants, auditors, computer specialists, and others, this agency is engaged in revenue management with no involvement in leasing, permitting, development, conservation, or other land management decisions.[105]

This section focuses on ONRR reported revenue for FY2013 for federal onshore areas in all states. For FY2013, ONRR reported a total of $4,296.9 million. These revenues were derived from federal lands located in 37 of the 50 states, as shown in **Table 19**. Revenues were derived from many energy and mineral commodities, including coal, gas, hardrock minerals, oil, phosphate, sodium, and sulfur.

Neither ONNR nor BLM—which issues and administers the leases on federal lands—breaks out the total reported revenue based on the agency administering the lands. Instead, agency records are organized by type of revenue, commodity, product, and other categories. Thus, statistics are not readily available on the portion of the revenues, if any, derived on lands managed by BLM, FWS, NPS, and FS, as well as other federal agencies.[106]

Federal energy and mineral revenue tend to vary widely from state to state (as well as from year to year). While there can be several reasons, a chief factor in state-to-state variations is the extent of federal acreage within a state and, of that acreage, the extent containing recoverable energy and mineral resources. For instance, as shown in **Table 19** and **Figure 11**, two states with relatively large federal acreage available for mineral exploration made up more than two-thirds (70.7%) of the total revenue reported for the nation. Each of these states—Wyoming and New Mexico— reported over a billion dollars in energy and mineral revenue from federal lands ($1,998.9 million and $1,040.8 million, respectively).

On the low end of the range of statistics considered, ONRR data show less than $1.0 million in onshore revenue for about half the states. These states had little or no mineral leasing activity during FY2013. In general, these states are among those with less extensive federal acreage and limited potential for energy and mineral development. Of the states in this category, there were no onshore receipts from 13 states: Connecticut, Delaware, Georgia, Hawaii, Iowa, Maine, Massachusetts, New Hampshire, New Jersey, Rhode Island, Tennessee, Vermont, and Wisconsin.[107] Further, several states had revenues less than $50,000,[108] with the lowest being North Carolina ($474), South Carolina ($4,440), and New York ($5,149).

In addition to the extent of federal acreage and related resource potential, other variables that could affect energy and mineral revenues are weather conditions (e.g., flooding, drought, or hurricane) and other special circumstances (e.g., forest fire or oil spill). Unplanned events, perhaps occurring over a prolonged period, could be a determinant of public revenue.[109] In the period considered, some states reported a variety of conditions contributing to changes in natural resource development.

Table 19. Office of Natural Resources Reported Revenues by State, FY2013 (in millions of dollars)

State	Revenue
Alabama	4.5
Alaska	22.0
Arizona	0.1
Arkansas	5.1
California	206.6
Colorado	294.7
Connecticut	0
Delaware	0
Florida	0.7
Georgia	0
Hawaii	0
Idaho	10.0
Illinois	0.3
Indiana	<0.1
Iowa	0
Kansas	5.4
Kentucky	1.9
Louisiana	12.5
Maine	0
Maryland	<0.1
Massachusetts	0
Michigan	1.5
Minnesota	0.1
Mississippi	6.1
Missouri	9.9
Montana	77.4
Nebraska	0.3
Nevada	16.1
New Jersey	0
New Mexico	1,040.8
New York	<0.1
North Carolina	<0.1
North Dakota	222.6

Table 19. (Continued)

State	Revenue
Ohio	0.4
Oklahoma	10.4
Oregon	0.6
Pennsylvania	0.1
Rhode Island	0
South Carolina	<0.1
South Dakota	2.3
Tennessee	0
Texas	34.2
Utah	310.7
Vermont	0
Virginia	0.2
Washington	<0.1
West Virginia	0.6
Wisconsin	0
Wyoming	1,998.9
Total	4,296.9

Source: Office of Natural Resources Revenue, Statistical Information, at http://statistics. Under "Common Data Summaries," see "All Reported Revenues." Specifically, the figures were derived as follows. The "Data Type" is "Reported Revenues (Single Year Only)," the "Year Type" is "Sales Year," the "Fiscal Year" is "FY2013," the "Land Category" is "Federal Onshore," and the "Geographic Area" is "All States" for the total shown and each individual state for state figures shown.

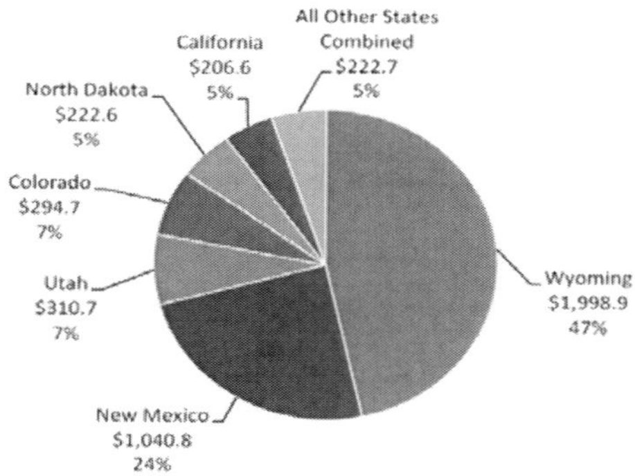

Source: Prepared by CRS with data from the Office of Natural Resources Revenue, Statistical Information, at http://statistics.

Figure 11. Office of Natural Resources Reported Revenue by State, FY2013; (in millions of dollars).

APPENDIX. FEDERAL ACREAGE IN EACH STATE ADMINISTERED BY THE FOUR MAJOR FEDERAL LAND MANAGEMENT AGENCIES, 2013

State	BLM	FWS	NPS	FS
Alabama	2,753	32,334	17,405	670,092
Alaska	72,363,733	76,673,836	52,431,579	22,207,400
Arizona	12,204,369	1,683,348	2,644,964	11,204,428
Arkansas	1,075	375,038	98,287	2,592,377
California	15,343,828	291,640	7,583,469	20,747,885
Colorado	8,335,703	174,230	661,472	14,482,727
Connecticut	0	1,522	5,719	23
Delaware	0	25,543	890	0
District of Columbia	0	0	6,975	0
Florida	351	281,986	2,469,065	1,193,051
Georgia	0	482,942	39,781	867,761
Hawaii	0	299,318a	357,814	0
Idaho	11,612,848	49,652	511,600	20,444,413
Illinois	0	89,765	12	304,480
Indiana	0	15,590	10,748	203,048
Iowa	0	71,490	2,708	0
Kansas	0	29,509	462	108,635
Kentucky	0	11,695	94,678	819,439
Louisiana	738	572,662	16,799	608,441
Maine	0	68,606	66,966	53,880
Maryland	548	48,100	41,041	0
Massachusetts	0	22,696	32,960	0
Michigan	0	115,692	631,846	2,873,920
Minnesota	1,447	503,560	139,571	2,844,476
Mississippi	5,020	210,894	104,015	1,191,774
Missouri	0	60,555	54,385	1,504,907
Montana	7,985,092	639,785	1,214,346	17,151,047
Nebraska	6,354	173,773	5,650	351,235
Nevada	47,782,464	2,345,956	774,751	5,759,160
New Hampshire	0	34,307	13,211	748,134
New Jersey	0	72,823	35,362	0
New Mexico	13,454,702	331,919	376,883	9,311,527
New York	0	28,768	33,703	16,352
North Carolina	0	420,068	363,483	1,254,557
North Dakota	58,970	487,941	71,258	1,103,162
Ohio	0	8,708	20,129	244,368
Oklahoma	1,975	106,728	10,008	400,146
Oregon	16,142,471	573,416	192,127	15,674,661
Pennsylvania	0	10,263	51,220	513,889
Rhode Island	0	2,415	5	0
South Carolina	0	127,657	31,972	630,991
South Dakota	274,522	206,498	147,028	2,006,319
Tennessee	0	54,093	358,797	718,674
Texas	11,833	547,117	1,204,897	756,910
Utah	22,853,486	109,805	2,097,756	8,187,926
Vermont	0	34,116	9,836	409,591

Appendix. (Continued)

State	BLM	FWS	NPS	FS
Virginia	805	130,188	304,825	1,662,875
Washington	429,083	150,024b	1,834,543	9,323,705
West Virginia	0	19,796	65,071	1,045,855
Wisconsin	2,324	201,742	61,744	1,523,487
Wyoming	18,375,734	70,677	2,344,972	9,214,708
U.S. Totalc	*247,252,228*	*89,080,785*	*79,648,788*	*192,932,426*
Territories	0	2,092,276	26,847	28,823
Marine Areas	0	209,774,187[d]	0	0
Agency Total	247,252,228	300,947,248d	79,675,635	192,961,249

Sources: For FS: U.S. Department of Agriculture, Forest Service, *Land Areas Report—As of Sept 30, 2013*, Tables 1 and 4, http://www.fs.fed.us/land/staff/lar/LAR2013/lar2013index.html. Data reflect land within the National Forest System, including national forests, national grasslands, purchase units, land utilization projects, experimental areas, and other areas. This source shows an agency total of 192,961,249 as reflected in this appendix. However, the individual state acreages in this source, and copied here, appear to sum to 192,961,259. The reason for the discrepancy is not apparent.

For NPS: U.S. Department of the Interior, National Park Service, Land Resources Division, *National Park Service, Listing of Acreage by State, as of 9/30/2013*, unpublished document. Data reflect federally owned lands managed by the NPS. For information on acreage by unit, see the NPS website, https://irma.nps.gov/Stats/.

For FWS: U.S. Department of the Interior, Fish and Wildlife Service, *Annual Report of Lands Under Control of the U.S. Fish and Wildlife Service, as of September 30, 2013*, Table 1A, http://www.fws.gov/refuges/land/PDF/2013_Annual_Report_of_Lands_Data_Tables.pdf. Data reflect all federally owned land over which the FWS has sole or primary jurisdiction.

For BLM: U.S. Dept. of the Interior, Bureau of Land Management, *Public Land Statistics, 2013*, Table 1-4, http://www.blm.gov/public_land_statistics/pls13/pls2013.pdf.

Notes: This table understates total federal land in each state because it includes only lands of the four major federal land management agencies, excluding the Department of Defense, Bureau of Reclamation, and other agencies.

[a] Excludes Papahanaumokuakea Marine National Monument (88,635,029 acres) administered by FWS.

[b] Includes Hanford Reach National Monument (32,965 acres) administered by FWS but not as part of the National Wildlife Refuge System.

[c] Includes only lands in the 50 states and the District of Columbia.

[d] Includes lands and waters of marine refuges and national monuments administered by FWS, both within and outside the National Wildlife Refuge System, including Papahanaumokuakea Marine National Monument (88,635,029 acres) northwest of Hawaii.

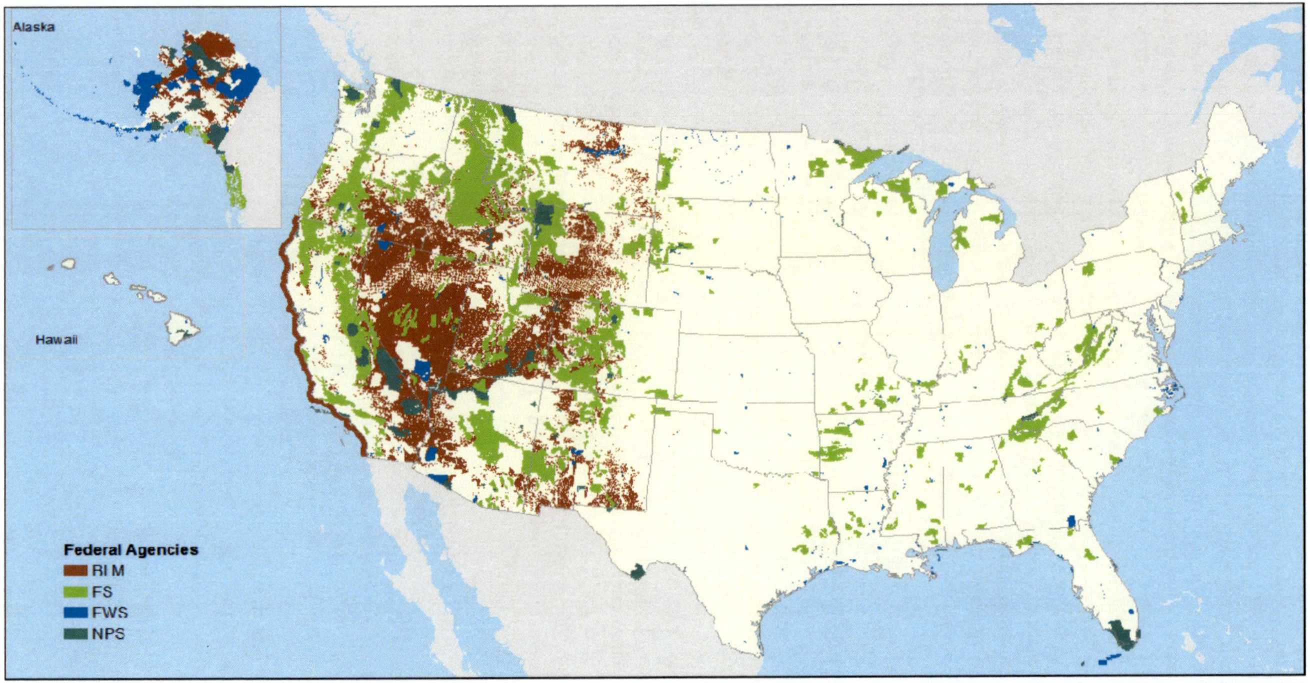

Source: Map boundaries and information generated by CRS using federal lands GIS data from the National Atlas, 2005, and ESRI USA Base Map.

Note: Inset maps are not to scale of the coterminous United States.

Figure A-1. Federal Lands by Agency: BLM, FWS, NPS, and FS.

End Notes

[1] For brief descriptions of these agencies, and an overview of current federal land issues, see CRS Report R43429, *Federal Lands and Natural Resources: Overview and Selected Issues for the 113th Congress*, coordinated by Katie Hoover.

[2] For some agencies and types of data, this report provides information for all 50 states. However, this is not the case for BLM appropriations and revenue, FWS revenue, NPS mandatory appropriations, and FS appropriations. Further, data are provided for the District of Columbia, territories, and other areas as applicable.

[3] Total federal land in the United States is not definitively known. In 2013, the four major federal land management agencies managed a total of 608.9 million acres in the United States. The total acreage managed by each of the four agencies, and the acreage in each state, are shown in the Appendix of this report. For historical information on acres managed by the four agencies and the Department of Defense, by state, see CRS Report R42346, *Federal Land Ownership: Overview and Data*, by Carol Hardy Vincent, Laura A. Hanson, and Marc R. Rosenblum.

[4] The Government Accountability Office (GAO) has analyzed the extent to which the four major federal land management agencies (and the Bureau of Reclamation) collect over 100 data elements related to lands and resources, revenues, and land use designations. The agency also reviewed how the agencies store these data elements, for instance, whether in a "primary agency data system," defined as a centralized electronic data system maintained at an agency-wide level; paper files; documents and files in multiple field locations; or other formats. Further, GAO assessed the "potential reliability" of the data elements that the agencies collected, determining that "less than half of the data elements stored in a primary agency data system were potentially reliable." For information on the extent to which land management agencies collect and make available data on lands, resources, and revenues, and the reliability of such data, see Government Accountability Office, *Federal Land Management: Availability and Potential Reliability of Selected Data Elements at Five Agencies*, GAO-12-691T, May 3, 2012, at http://www.gao.gov/assets. The text quoted in this footnote is from p. 12 of this GAO document.

[5] Public sources include agency websites, agency budget justifications, and other sources that CRS could access directly.

[6] This presented varying degrees of challenge for the agencies for several reasons. For example, the agencies generally do not collect and maintain data by state in the manner sought and presented in this report. In some cases the agencies extrapolated the information needed from data sources maintained for differing purposes and in varying formats. However, this was not always possible. For instance, the NPS was not able to break out mandatory appropriations by state, and the agencies were not able to identify each agency's portion of mineral leasing revenues reported by ONRR. In general, this CRS report does not analyze the quality or comprehensiveness of the agency data presented.

[7] The amount of appropriations for the land management agencies to use in a particular state is not contained in sources available to the public. As a result, CRS obtained most of the appropriations figures for this report directly from BLM, FWS, NPS, and FS. For each agency, we sought to obtain the total appropriations for each state. We also requested that the agencies distinguish between discretionary and mandatory portions. Further, we asked for appropriations by account. The amount of revenue derived by BLM, FWS, and NPS in each state also is not available in public sources. As a result, CRS obtained information for

this report directly from these agencies. However, FS revenue by state is available on the agency's website, as noted in the "Forest Service" section of this report.

[8] As noted in Table 3, BLM's appropriated entitlements are reflected here as mandatory appropriations. In the case of appropriated entitlements, the level of spending is controlled by authorizing statutes but the funding is provided in appropriations acts. For additional information on the distinction between discretionary and mandatory appropriations, and on other aspects of the appropriations and budgetary processes, see CRS Report R42388, *The Congressional Appropriations Process: An Introduction*, by Jessica Tollestrup, and CRS Report 98-721, *Introduction to the Federal Budget Process*, coordinated by Bill Heniff, Jr.

[9] FS data on mandatory appropriations also may reflect some carry-over funds, as noted in the Forest Service section of this report.

[10] Appropriations are available to be obligated for differing time periods. While some appropriations are provided for one fiscal year only, others are provided for longer periods. In these cases, appropriations may be carried over from one fiscal year to the next and remain available for obligation until the end of the last fiscal year (for multiyear appropriations) or until expended (for appropriations without fiscal year limitation). Many of the accounts for the four land management agencies receive appropriations that can be obligated in multiple fiscal years.

[11] As an example, using total BLM budget authority would result in significantly different estimates of BLM funding in Nevada. Most notably, the total FY2013 budget authority in the special account established under the Southern Nevada Public Land Management Act of 1998 (SNPLMA) was $484.9 million, according to BLM. Nearly all of the money in the account was from the sale of BLM lands in Clark County, NV, prior to FY2013. The new FY2013 budget authority derived from these sales was only $10.5 million, as shown in Table 3 below.

[12] According to the Government Accountability Office, an obligation is a "definite commitment that creates a legal liability of the government for the payment of goods and services ordered or received, or a legal duty on the part of the United States that could mature into a legal liability." An expenditure is "the actual spending of money; an outlay." These definitions are taken from: U.S. Government Accountability Office, *A Glossary of Terms Used in the Federal Budget Process*, September 2005, pp. 48 and 70.

[13] As an example, using obligation figures rather than new budget authority would result in significantly different estimates of BLM funding in Nevada. The FY2013 obligation from the Southern Nevada Public Land Management Act account was $158.5 million, according to BLM. These obligations were from amounts collected in prior fiscal years. As noted, the new FY2013 budget authority was $10.5 million.

[14] Additional information on appropriations for the land management agencies is included in other CRS reports. For instance, information on FY2015 appropriations for the four agencies, among others, is contained in CRS Report R43617, Interior, Environment, and Related Agencies: FY2015 Appropriations, by Carol Hardy Vincent, and on FY2013 and FY2014 appropriations is in CRS Report R43142, *Interior, Environment, and Related Agencies: FY2013 and FY2014 Appropriations*, by Carol Hardy Vincent. For information on appropriations for the Fish and Wildlife Service, see CRS Report R43678, *Fish and Wildlife Service: FY2015 Appropriations and Policy*, by M. Lynne Corn; for the National Park Service, see CRS Report R42757, *National Park Service: Recent Appropriations Trends*, by Laura B. Comay; for the Forest Service, see CRS Report R43417, *Forest Service Appropriations, FY2010-FY2014: In Brief*, by Katie Hoover; and on wildland fire

management, see CRS Report R43077, *Wildfire Management: Federal Funding and Related Statistics*, by Kelsi Bracmort.

[15] CRS obtained the state-by-state FHWA distributions directly from the agency, as they are not publicly available.

[16] The PILT data used in this report are from the DOI website. The SRS data were drawn from both agency websites (DOI and FS) as well as directly from the FS. The "Payment Programs" section below identifies the specific sources.

[17] Mineral leasing revenues reported by ONRR were derived from the agency's website, as presented below under "Office of Natural Resources Revenue."

[18] P.L. 113-2, the Disaster Relief Appropriations Act, 2013, provided supplemental appropriations for numerous departments and agencies, including FWS, NPS, and FS. For an overview of the amounts and purposes of the appropriations, see CRS Report R42869, *FY2013 Supplemental Funding for Disaster Relief*, coordinated by William L. Painter and Jared T. Brown.

[19] For an overview of the FY2013 sequester, see CRS Report R42949, *The American Taxpayer Relief Act of 2012: Modifications to the Budget Enforcement Procedures in the Budget Control Act*, by Bill Heniff, Jr.

[20] The operation of the "Helium Production Fund" is addressed in 50 U.S.C. §167a(c)) and §167 d(e). The name assigned to the fund by the Office of Management and Budget and the U.S. Treasury is the "Helium Fund." Thus, the two terms refer to the same fund.

[21] However, the FHWA could not identify $82.9 million by state, so this amount is not reflected in the state totals discussed here.

[22] In addition, Puerto Rico received a payment of less than $2.0 million.

[23] This total includes a $478.1 million allocation from DOI's Wildland Fire Management account. However, it excludes a total of $2.6 million in allocations from several other accounts outside BLM, such as the Forest Service's State and Private Forestry account. Also, as noted in the introduction to this report, this figure represents *new* FY2013 budget authority. *Total* BLM budget authority for FY2013 would be larger, due to the carry-over of funds from prior fiscal years. Most notably, the total FY2013 budget authority in the special account established under the Southern Nevada Public Land Management Act of 1998 (SNPLMA) was $484.9 million. Nearly all of the money in the account was from the sale of BLM lands in Clark County, NV prior to FY2013. The new FY2013 budget authority derived from these sales was only $10.5 million, as shown in Table 3, below.

[24] A primary exception is appropriations derived from BLM land sales under SNPLMA. The majority of proceeds (85%) of these land disposals are deposited into a special account. The proceeds in the special account are used for the benefit of multiple agencies, including BLM, FWS, NPS, and FS. Further, the remaining 15% of the proceeds from BLM land sales under SNPLMA are not used on BLM lands; these funds are paid to the state of Nevada and the Southern Nevada Water Authority.

[25] For information on appropriations over time for managing wildfires and for statistics on wildfires, see CRS Report R43077, *Wildfire Management: Federal Funding and Related Statistics*, by Kelsi Bracmort.

[26] For information on Oregon and California grant lands, including management, federal payments to O&C counties, and issues for Congress, see CRS Report R42951, *The Oregon and California Railroad Lands (O&C Lands): Issues for Congress*, by Katie Hoover.

[27] The fund is credited with payments from appropriations, and funds from BLM and other agencies and sources, for the cost of furnishing supplies, equipment, facilities, and services. The appropriations are classified as discretionary.

The authority to spend is based on collections credited to the fund in a particular year, which were $62.4 million in FY2013, according to the BLM Budget Office.

[28] An interest in land is something less than full ownership, such as a conservation easement or mineral rights.

[29] Under current law, 50 U.S.C. §167d, revenues in excess of amounts needed to operate the helium program are paid to the General Fund of the U.S. Treasury.

[30] For information on the Secure Rural Schools and Community Self-Determination Act of 2000, including its relationship with other compensation programs, legislative history, and issues for Congress, see CRS Report R41303, *Reauthorizing the Secure Rural Schools and Community Self-Determination Act of 2000*, by Katie Hoover.

[31] For the acreage of land managed by BLM in each state, see the **Appendix** of this report. These statistics were taken from Bureau of Land Management, *Public Land Statistics, 2013*, Table 1-4, at http://www.blm.gov/public_land_statistics/pls13/pls2013.pdf. For the acreage of onshore federal mineral estate managed by BLM in each state, see Table 1-3 in *Public Land Statistics, 2013.*

[32] This is because while the helium is stored in Texas, BLM does not have a separate Texas state office. Instead, the New Mexico state office administers BLM lands and onshore mineral resources in Texas. Although sold by BLM, the helium is not produced by BLM.

[33] This statement excludes the $297.3 million appropriation for "no state," which was higher than the appropriation for Oregon.

[34] The only BLM Secure Rural Schools payment was made to Oregon, with an additional $0.2 million for "no state" in FY2013.

[35] This total excludes "Undistributed Intergovernmental Payments" because they are transfers between accounts, not revenues collected by BLM.

[36] Locatable minerals include metallic minerals (e.g., gold, silver, copper), nonmetallic minerals (e.g., mica and gypsum), and other minerals generally found in the subsurface. Developing these minerals on federal lands is guided by the General Mining Law of 1872. The law grants free access to individuals and corporations to prospect for minerals in open public domain lands and allows them, upon making a discovery, to stake (or "locate") a claim on the deposit.

[37] This is the case even though the helium is produced in multiple states and stored in Texas. The New Mexico state office administers BLM lands and resources in Texas, as noted above.

[38] The appropriations figures in this report differ slightly from the FY2013 estimates shown in *U.S. Department of the Interior, Budget Justifications and Performance Information, Fiscal Year 2015, Fish and Wildlife Service*, at http://www.fws.gov/budget /2014/FY2015_ FWS_Greenbook-DOI31014.pdf. The figures in this report reflect the most recent data and were provided by Chris Nolin, Budget Division, Fish and Wildlife Service, on July 18, 2014.

[39] This estimate was determined by CRS as follows. First, certain accounts are not spent on FWS lands: State and Tribal Wildlife Grants, Cooperative Endangered Species Conservation Fund, North American Wetlands Conservation Account, Multinational Species Conservation Fund, Neotropical Migratory Bird Conservation Fund, Wildlife Restoration, and Sportfish Restoration; in FY2013, they totaled $1,123.3 million. Second, some major subaccounts within the Resource Management account are spent largely or entirely outside of refuge lands: Endangered Species; Habitat Conservation; Environmental Contaminants; Conservation, Enforcement, and Science; and General Operations; these subaccounts totaled $572.3 million. Third, other accounts have variable percents spent on FWS lands: Wildland Fire Management, Contributed Funds, National Wildlife Refuge Fund, and

Miscellaneous Permanent Appropriations; these accounts totaled $84.1 million. Consequently, while FWS cannot provide a precise estimate, CRS estimates the total spent off of the NWRS at about two-thirds of the agency's spending. By contrast, some account-level programs are spent only on FWS lands: Construction, Land Acquisition, Migratory Bird Conservation Account, and Recreation Fee Enhancement Program. For more on FWS accounts and their purposes, see text below as well as CRS Report R43678, *Fish and Wildlife Service: FY2015 Appropriations and Policy*, by M. Lynne Corn.

[40] For example, under P.L. 113-2, $64.6 million in FY2013 supplemental Construction funding was provided to Delaware and New Jersey in the wake of Superstorm Sandy.

[41] The total of $34.1 million includes $0.5 million in mandatory appropriations.

[42] For an overview of the NWRF, see CRS Report R42404, *Fish and Wildlife Service: Compensation to Local Governments*, by M. Lynne Corn. Details regarding NWRF funding were provided by Cathy Deamer, FWS Budget Office, October 20, 2014.

[43] In addition, in FY2013, $8.0 million was collected in gross receipts for activities on wildlife refuges. This amount became available without further appropriation for expenditure in FY2014. Some will be used to offset costs of managing revenue-generating programs and the remainder for payment to local governments.

[44] For additional information on these two funds, see CRS Report RS21157, *International Species Conservation Funds*, by Pervaze A. Sheikh and M. Lynne Corn.

[45] For more information on these two programs, see http://wsfrprograms.fws.gov/home.html.

[46] For more information on the MBCA, see http://www.fws.gov/refuges/realty/mbcc.html.

[47] These revenues are not included in the totals in the section below on "Revenue."

[48] For the acreage of land managed by FWS, see the Appendix of this report. These statistics were taken from *Statistical Data Tables for Lands Under Control of the Fish and Wildlife Service (as of 9/30/2013)*, on the FWS website at http://www.fws.gov/refuges/land/LandReport.html. Data for earlier fiscal years also are at this site.

[49] The FY2013 total does not include fines under various laws, such as the Lacey Act (18 U.S.C. §42). It was derived from *U.S. Department of the Interior, Budget Justifications and Performance Information, Fiscal Year 2015, Fish and Wildlife Service*, at http://www.fws.gov/budget/2014/FY2015_FWS_Greenbook-DOI31014.pdf. This source provides additional information on the various programs mentioned here.

[50] See 16 U.S.C. §668dd. Note that some economic activity may occur in the NWRS and generate revenue, but not for FWS. Examples may include preexisting energy or mineral rights. This section reflects only receipts collected by FWS.

[51] In some instances, FWS lacks discretion to reduce or eliminate commercial activities. Examples include split estates, in which some other entity owns subsurface rights to energy or mineral resources; secondary FWS jurisdiction, where some other federal agency has primary jurisdiction; and the presence of easements or leases.

[52] In some FWS regions, collections are used only at the site where they were collected. Other regions hold up to 20% of collections from a site for distribution to other, less-visited sites in the same region in the following year.

[53] For more information on these programs, see Miscellaneous Permanent Appropriations in *U.S. Department of the Interior, Budget Justifications and Performance Information, Fiscal Year 2015, Fish and Wildlife Service*, at http://www.fws.gov/budget/2014/FY2015_FWS_Greenbook-DOI31014.pdf.

[54] This total includes $110.2 million allocated to NPS from a DOI-wide account for Wildland Fire Management. If the Wildland Fire allocation were not included, the total discretionary appropriation would be $2,774.9 million. The total includes a supplemental appropriation of

$377.3 million for disaster relief under P.L. 113-2, and also reflects a $30 million rescission of contract authority from the Land and Water Conservation Fund. The figures shown here and in Table 8 for discretionary appropriations are based on personal communication with the NPS Budget Office, September-November 2014.

[55] The total for FY2013 mandatory appropriations is drawn from National Park Service, *Budget Justifications and Performance Information, Fiscal Year 2015*, p. Overview-5, at http://www.nps.gov/aboutus/upload/FY-2015- Greenbook-Linked.pdf, hereinafter referred to as NPS FY2015 budget justification.

56 NPS also received funding from other department-wide or other agency accounts: DOI's Central Hazardous Materials Fund; DOI's Natural Resource Damage Assessment and Restoration Fund; DOI's Office of the Secretary, Departmental Operations account; BLM's Southern Nevada Public Lands Management account; FS's State and Private Forestry account; and two Federal Highway Administration accounts. These allocations are not reflected in Table 8. Tables in this report for other agencies (e.g., BLM and FS) may reflect some of these monies.

[57] All percentages in this section are derived from the total discretionary appropriation, before the $30 million rescission of Land and Water Conservation Fund contract authority.

[58] This figure shows the supplemental Construction appropriation after sequestration.

[59] This figure shows the supplemental HPF appropriation after sequestration. The supplemental funding resulted in a higher HPF total for eastern states such as New York and New Jersey than would have been appropriated by formula (see Table 8).

[60] For more information on the LWCF, see CRS Report RL33531, *Land and Water Conservation Fund: Overview, Funding History, and Issues*, by Carol Hardy Vincent.

[61] For more information on national heritage areas, see CRS Report RL33462, *Heritage Areas: Background, Proposals, and Current Issues*, by Carol Hardy Vincent and Laura B. Comay.

[62] The 16 mandatory appropriations were the Recreation Fee Program; Concessions Franchise Fees; Contribution for Annuity Benefits for U.S. Park Police; Donations; Operation and Maintenance of Quarters; Transportation Systems Fund; Concessions Improvement Accounts; Park Buildings Lease and Maintenance Fund; Glacier Bay National Park Resource Protection; Deed Restricted Parks Fee Program; Filming and Photography Special Use Fee Program; Educational Expenses for Children of Employees at Yellowstone National Park; Outer Continental Shelf Oil Lease Revenues; Delaware Water Gap National Recreation Area Route 209 Operations; Payment for Tax Losses on Land Acquired for Grand Teton National Park; and Preservation of the Birthplace of Abraham Lincoln. The mandatory total of $420.6 million also includes Land and Water Conservation Fund contract authority of $30 million, although this authority was rescinded in FY2013 in P.L. 113-6. See NPS FY2015 budget justification, p. Overview-38.

[63] For example, mandatory appropriations from the Treasury for annuity benefits to U.S. Park Police are not included in Table 9.

[64] 16 U.S.C. §§6801-6814. FLREA applies to five federal agencies. For background, see CRS Report RL33730, *Recreation Fees Under the Federal Lands Recreation Enhancement Act*, by Carol Hardy Vincent.

[65] In general, the law (16 U.S.C. §6806) provides for at least 80% of fees to be used at the collecting site, although the Interior Secretary may reduce this amount to as little as 60% if the revenue collected exceeds the unit's reasonable needs. In FY2013, the majority of NPS units retained 80% of collected recreation fees, and parks collecting less than $500,000 in recreation fees retained 100%.

[66] The amount reflects sequestration and includes both the Recreation Fee Program and the Deed Restricted Parks Fee Program. The latter program involves Great Smoky Mountains National Park (Tennessee and North Carolina), Lincoln Home National Historic Site (IL), and Abraham Lincoln Birthplace National Historic Site (KY), where entrance fees cannot be collected because of deed restrictions. Other types of recreation fees are collected at these parks.

[67] 16 U.S.C. §§5951-5966, National Park Service Concessions Management Improvement Act of 1998.

[68] However, for the first half of FY2013, there was no park unit in Delaware; see Table 8. The state of Delaware nonetheless received some NPS appropriations in FY2013, such as through the Historic Preservation Fund.

[69] For the acreage of land managed by NPS, see the Appendix of this report.

[70] Some other NPS appropriations—for example, for NPS Construction, and National Recreation and Preservation— were not as widely distributed, reaching only certain states and territories in FY2013.

[71] For example, the NPS maintains a police force, the U.S. Park Police, for three urban areas—New York, San Francisco, and Washington, DC.

[72] The NPS has seven regional offices, located in Alaska, California, Colorado, Nebraska, Pennsylvania, Georgia, and Washington, DC. Washington, DC, is also where the agency has its headquarters. Washington, DC, received the most NPS appropriations ($857.2 million) of any location in FY2013.

[73] Personal communication with NPS budget office, September-November 2014.

[74] As discussed above, not all NPS revenues collected within a state necessarily stay within that state, so the revenue amounts do not match the state's mandatory appropriation from a given account. A state's mandatory appropriation from a revenue program such as the Recreation Fee Program or the Concession Franchise Fee Program could be either less or more than the amount of revenues collected in that state. The appropriation could be less because some of the collected fees were placed in a central NPS account, rather than being retained in the state. A state's mandatory appropriation from the program could also be more than was collected—for example, if a state whose parks collected no recreation or concession fees had monies allocated to it from the central funds.

[75] The other sources primarily included $39.3 million in direct donations to the parks. In Table 9, these donations are shown in the "Unallocated geography" row, since the agency does not track its donations by state. Another source is the Filming and Photography Special Use Fee Program, which collects fees from commercial filmmakers and photographers. These revenues were collected in many states but totaled a relatively small amount (less than $1 million). Other sources are specific to a single park unit.

[76] For the acreage of land managed by FS in each state, see the Appendix of this report. These statistics were taken from Forest Service, *Land Areas Report (LAR)-as of September 30, 2013*, Table 4, at http://www.fs.fed.us/land/staff/lar/LAR2013/lar2013index.html.

[77] For a complete list of the National Forest System units by region or by state, see Forest Service, *Land Areas Report*, September 30, 2013, at http://www.fs.fed.us/land/staff/lar/LAR2013/lar2013index.html.

[78] See Table 5, Forest Service, *Land Areas Report*, September 30, 2013, at http://www.fs.fed.us/land/staff/lar/LAR2013/lar2013index.html.

[79] In addition to the nine FS regions, the FS allocates appropriations to five research stations, two service centers and laboratories located throughout the United States, and the national headquarters office in Washington, DC.

[80] In addition to the reasons discussed here, estimates are further complicated by a change during FY2013 in the Forest Service's accounting software, according to the agency. Personal communication between CRS and Forest Service Budget Office, April 2014.

[81] 16 U.S.C. §576-576b. K-V revenue is derived from timber sale receipts. The Forest Service is authorized to retain a portion of timber and salvage timber sale receipts in a special fund (the K-V fund) to pay for certain specified projects on the timber sale area. The K-V fund may also be called the Cooperative Work Knutson-Vandenburg, or CWKV, fund.

[82] Combined, revenue or collections associated with timber or salvage timber sales accounted for $129.5 million (57.9%) of the total revenue generated on national forest lands. The combined timber revenue includes revenue from timber sales, salvage timber sales, KV fund deposits, Timber Sale Pipeline Restoration fund deposits, and certain credits or deposits timber sale contract purchasers make for road construction purposes. The Forest Service tracks these receipts separately, due in part to statutory mandates governing the disposition of those receipts, either to the general treasury or retained by the Forest Service for various specified purposes.

[83] U.S. Department of Transportation, Federal Highway Administration, *America's Highways, 1776-1976: A History of the Federal-Aid Program* (Washington, DC: Government Printing Office, 1976), p. 486. FHWA was formerly the Office of Road Inquiry, the Office of Public Roads, the Bureau of Public Roads, and the Public Roads Administration.

[84] 23 U.S.C. §201 et seq.

[85] P.L. 113-159.

[86] For information on the changes made by MAP-21 to federal lands and tribal transportation programs, see CRS Report R42762, *Surface Transportation Funding and Programs Under MAP-21: Moving Ahead for Progress in the 21st Century Act (P.L. 112-141)*, coordinated by Robert S. Kirk.

[87] The Office of Federal Lands Highway also administers the Tribal Transportation Program, which is not considered here.

[88] MAP-21 provides contract authority, a type of budget authority, for the Federal-Aid Highway Program (FAHP), including the Federal Lands Highway Program. MAP-21 makes these funds, drawn from the Highway Trust Fund, available for obligation without further legislative action. To control the flow of funds from the Highway Trust Fund, a limit is placed on the total obligations that can be entered into involving the FAHP during a fiscal year. This is known as an obligation limitation.

[89] Based on lands managed by the BLM, FWS, NPS, FS, and Corps.

[90] SAFETEA-LU (P.L. 109-59), the predecessor to MAP-21.

[91] For an overview of the program, see 23 U.S.C. §125 and the FHWA website on the program at http://flh.fhwa.dot.gov/programs/erfo/.

[92] Another $7.6 million was distributed to other agencies that are not the focus of this report (e.g., U.S. Army Corps of Engineers), for a total of $581.4 million.

[93] A state PDC is required to make project funding decisions using FLAP distributions. A state PDC must be composed of three members, representing FHWA, the state department of transportation, and an appropriate political subdivision of the state (23 U.S.C. §204).

[94] For an overview of programs to compensate state and local governments for the tax-exempt status of federal lands, and related issues, see CRS Report R42439, *Compensating State and Local Governments for the Tax-Exempt Status of Federal Lands: What Is Fair and Consistent?*, by M. Lynne Corn.

[95] 31 U.S.C. §§6901-6907.

[96] *Payments in Lieu of Taxes: National Summary*, FY2013, at http://www.doi.gov/pilt/upload/2013_PILT_AnnualReport.pdf.

[97] *Payments in Lieu of Taxes: National Summary*, FY2013. The 16 counties were in eight states: Alaska (1), Arizona (3), California (3), Colorado (1), Nevada (2), New Mexico (1), Utah (3), and Wyoming (2).

[98] Mandatory spending for PILT was authorized through FY2014. As mandatory spending, no appropriation in the annual appropriation law was required. For more on the PILT program, see CRS Report RL31392, *PILT (Payments in Lieu of Taxes): Somewhat Simplified*, by M. Lynne Corn.

[99] 16 U.S.C. §§7101-7153.

[100] The SRS program expired at the end of FY2013. For additional information on the SRS program, see CRS Report R41303, *Reauthorizing the Secure Rural Schools and Community Self-Determination Act of 2000*, by Katie Hoover.

[101] The FS maintains state-, county-, and forest-level data on these payments at http://www.fs.usda.gov/main/pts/securepayments/projectedpayments.

[102] A bonus is the "cash consideration paid to the United States by the successful bidder for a mineral lease." U.S. Department of the Interior, *Public Land Statistics 2013*, p. 252, available on the BLM website at http://www.blm.gov/public_land_statistics/pls13/pls2013.pdf.

[103] A rent is the obligation to pay an annual amount to maintain the development rights on a lease.

[104] A royalty is the obligation to pay, on an annual basis, a percentage of the produced value associated with the lease.

[105] For a comprehensive description of ONRR's accounting and audit mission and workforce, see http://www.onrr.gov/About/faqs.htm.

[106] Reported revenue, if any, from activities on federal lands other than those managed by BLM, FWS, NPS, and FS is outside the scope of this report.

[107] In Tennessee, use of federal lands is governed in part by the Tennessee Valley Authority Act (16 U.S.C. §831, et seq.). This act created the Tennessee Valley Authority (TVA) to manage options for energy and other development operations on federal lands in the state. TVA revenue reporting provisions were originally enacted as part of the Public Utility Holding Company Act of 1935 and now can be found in multiple federal statutes.

[108] These figure are shown in the table as <$0.1.

[109] See, for example, CRS Report R43396, *The Hurricane Sandy Rebuilding Strategy: In Brief*, by Jared T. Brown.

INDEX

A

B

C

F

G

H

N

O

P

Q

R

S

T

U

V

W

Y